END THE MENTAL STIGMA

Researcher/Analyst

Contents

This book is mainly to create awareness about the challenges people with mental illness and their caregivers face. This compilation of interviews gives a range of insights from sufferers and contributes to further understanding their world. People working in the psychology sector or mental health field may also find this book beneficial as the stories reveal the truth behind the lives of people with mental illness. I hope this book leads not only to increased awareness but also to help create strategies for us to live better lives.

Acknowledgement

I am very thankful to Jennifer Mapara for helping me edit this book. I am also thankful to Abhishek Austin and Vijay Nallawala for their contribution to the book.

Thanks to all the participants for their involvement and giving valuable information to enlighten every soul.

P.S: Answers have not been grammatically checked or proof read. The responses will appear exactly as they were conveyed by participants.

Introduction

Terms (created by me to simplify the language):
Ordered People: Who don't have any kind of mental illness
Disordered People: Who have mental illness.

The purpose of these interviews is to find the missing thread between disordered and ordered people (who don't have mental illness). Psychologists and other professionals work hard to educate people however there is lack of awareness of mental illnesses in the community. Through these interviews it is interesting to observe that a 24 year old and 68 year old suffering from mental illness have similar thoughts and agree that lack of awareness is a major issue in understanding, treating and living with an illness. The interviews reveal many areas where there are knowledge gaps and the very real and urgent need to reconsider our approach towards mentally disordered people. One important issue is that in the Hindi language, there are no words for Bipolar Disorder or Schizophrenia or Borderline Personality Disorder so it's very hard for an Indian to accept the psychology. Another factor in India is that many people are superstitious which leads to further misunderstanding and discrimination. One challenge is therefore to think about how to make these words are understood and accepted in the community. Another very important aspect is that people with mental health challenges should aim to help themselves as much as possible using a variety of strategies, because dependency can result in frustration, anger and other negative lifestyle side effects.

What makes disordered people different from ordered people?

Nearly 1 million people commit suicide every year worldwide . Since the late 19th century we have been looking for solutions to psychological disorders by treating them with medications and therapy.

The purpose of this study is to look into the minds of disordered people to find the areas to focus on to further understanding the disorders, and also develop appropriate coping strategies.

One of the main obstacles for people suffering from mental disorders is to communicate effectively with the "outside world" (ordered people). Difficulties can occur with communication and social skills, which in turn can cause related behavioral and mood problems.

How is it affecting our lives?

Some of the areas of life that can be affected include getting and maintaining a job or careers, , maintaining physical well-being, studying, financial status. Mental health can also greatly affect relationships and family life. In India superstitions can affect many people causing a negative or positive influence on someone with a mental health problem.

What affects mental health?

Everyone is unique and we all are living different lives and facing different circumstances. There are a number of factors in life that can have an impact on our mental health: childhood abuse, loneliness, experiencing discrimination, having a long-term physical health condition, domestic violence, poverty, debt, unemployment and many other reasons.

CHAPTER 1

Participant: *Mentally ill*
Age: *36*
Gender: *Male*
City: *Mumbai*
Occupation: *Poet/Solo Backpacker*

Q1) What are you suffering from?

Answer: Bipolar Disorder.

Q2) How did you get to know about it, is there any story you want to share?

Answer: It was 2004. I was in third year of my Engineering Undergraduate course. In 5th semester. We had a course Presentation and Communication Skills. Out of nowhere, I had started getting fear of this course. It resulted in a Major Depression Episode and I got hospitalized. Then there were rounds of meeting psychiatrists, medicines and ECTs. Psychiatrists treated me for major depression and there was no psychotherapy. After a couple of years of stable mood, when a manic episode occurred, then I was hospitalized again in a different hospital. Then after looking at my medical history and symptoms, doctors concluded it's not just Depression, but it's Bipolar Disorder.

Q3) How long has it been?

Answer: It has been 16 years, since I had my first episode. I have survived a couple of Depression and manic episodes.

Q4) Are you on medication?

Answer: Yes

Q5) How is it affecting your life?

Answer: It affects my decision making abilities. I most of the time get confused about what's right and what's wrong for my existence.

Q6) How is your work life?

Answer: I couldn't keep my jobs stable because Episodes occurred in Bipolar Disorder. I would either resign or I would get fired. So I don't really know where my work life headed and which career will suit me.

Q7) What do you think that ordered people don't understand?

Answer: They have stigma about people having mental illness. I myself can give an example. I wanted to have a companion for life so when I created a matrimonial profile and mentioned my mental illness, I got rejected by most of the girls.

Q8) Do you want to convey any particular message to the ordered people?

Answer: A fractured body part can heal with a cast but a fractured mind needs compassion and tender emotions like love and empathy. Please don't generalize us in one word. "MENTAL" or "PAGAL".

Q9) What do you think that psychology as a sector needs to develop?

Answer: Psychologists should keep a human centric approach and should not search money making medium in every patient they treat.

Q10) Do you have any creative things that you have written and you want it to get published?

Answer:

My mental illness and I
My mental illness and I
We talk with each other...
It's not cough or fever but,
It's Bipolar Mood Disorder...

It all had begun in 2004,
All of sudden out of nowhere...
Depression and suicidal thoughts,
Entire semester ECTs, tablets
and I got bedridden...

If it's a physical disability,
No one will make fun...
But mental illness is invisible,
Stigmatized very often...

It's episode of
depression or mania,
Pain is there for my family...
When will I recover is
the question for my

sisters, friends and आई...

Wait, let me tell you about
My Life with Bipolar Disorder...
It's been patches of rain in sunny days,
A Crazy hollywood movie with rainbow colors, twists
and turns...

I have been thinking one day,
I will open up to the world...
I will write a poetry about
my mental illness,
Hoping that society won't judge...

I hope you have not... :-)

CHAPTER 2

Participant: *Mentally ill*
Age: *43*
Gender: *Female*
City: *Delhi*
Occupation: *Self Employed*

Q1) What are you suffering from?

Answer: Bipolar-2.

Q2) How did you get to know about it, is there any story you want to share?

Answer: October 2019 I suffered a hypomanic episode. My first known episode in 43 years! Did not know I was suffering from Bipolar until the episode. Lasted several months of extreme high energy, high confidence, when usually I was socially shy, lacking judgement in certain situations. Got diagnosed in December 2019. Was very happy to be diagnosed but at the same time a little concerned for my future. My mother also has Bipolar.

Q3) How long has it been?

Answer: Diagnosed in December 2019 but now aware of this being a lifelong affliction.

Q4) Are you on medication?

Answer: No.

Q5) How is it affecting your life?

Answer: It has made me feel less guilty about myself and my actions. I thought I was lazy and unmotivated all these years. Did not know I was suffering from an illness. Also my lack of control over my emotions is now understood.

Q6) How is your work life?

Answer: Work life is OK now as I'm self employed. I have suffered over the years at various jobs keeping work relationships steady. Also have had periods of unemployment due to fatigue (which was probably the depressive phase of bipolar).

Q7) What do you think that ordered people don't understand?

Answer: It's very difficult for people who are not suffering from this to understand, medical professionals included. Knowing that you have certain mood and thought problems makes it an invisible problem. People cannot relate to the effect mood and emotions and thinking can have on our everyday lives. It's not a small problem - it affects almost every part of our life and can continue to do so unless we approach it differently. Bipolar does not mean we are stupid or lacking in abilities or dangerous or untrustworthy. Unfortunately this is what some people think of mentally ill people.

Q8) Do you want to convey any particular message to the ordered people?

Answer: Please try and treat us the same as anyone.... Everyone has problems, ours are different to yours that's all. Treat us the same :). Before I was diagnosed I was one of the most trusted, responsible and mature people in my family and amongst my friends. After diagnosis some of their opinions changed sadly.

Q9) What do you think that psychology as a sector needs to develop?

Answer: I think there is an enormous problem in this field. I think the current treatments are too centred around things we sometimes struggle to control (mainly our thoughts). I think the psychologists can cause stress when asking the client /patient to change too much. I don't believe we have to adjust that much. I feel many problems we face are related to employment and social issues. These are areas that the psychologist could assist with. These actually make a difference to our lives.

Q10) Do you have any creative things that you have written and you want it to get published?

Answer: Unfortunately not. I wish I was creative :)

CHAPTER 3

Participant: *Mentally ill*
Age: *19*
Gender: *Male*
City: *Mumbai*
Occupation: *Student*

Q1) What are you suffering from?

Answer: I'm suffering from bipolar ii disorder.

Q2) How did you get to know about it, is there any story you want to share?

Answer: I got to know about it by a self trigger. I wasn't able to study well or concentrate on class. Even if i concentrate i couldn't grasp what i was taught. This led to a trigger where I was diagnosed as anxiety disorder. Later on after a year and half I came to know that it was bipolar disorder.

Q3) How long has it been?

Answer: It has been around 3years and 5 months.

Q4) Are you on medication?

Answer: Yes im medication right from the day i was diagnosed and had a trigger.

Q5) How is it affecting your life?

Answer: I had to take a year gap for my studies because I wasn't able to study and it was a stressor for me and it made the disorder worse.

Q6) How is your work life?

Answer: Well my work life was difficult because the disorder was causing a lot of inconsistencies in work.

Q7) What do you think that ordered people don't understand?

Answer: The disorder itself is unique and people think it can be cured and it doesn't affect a person."The person needs to be strong, u can get over it, " are many common comments i had received.

Q8) Do you want to convey any particular message to the ordered people?

Answer: If you find any person with such disorder always express empathy and help him all the way u can. And don't give unsolicited advice to them.And don't judge them.

Q9) What do you think that psychology as a sector needs to develop?

Answer: The doctors need to give more time to patients and try to make them feel safe and have a patient doctor suitable ratio.

Q10) Do you have any creative things that you have written and you want it to get published?

Answer: No i haven't done anything creative.

CHAPTER 4

Participant: *Mentally ill*
Age: *39*
Gender: *Male*
City: *Mumbai*
Occupation: *Lawyer*

Q1) What are you suffering from?

Answer: I am diagnosed with Bipolar Mood Disorder and I suffer from the same.

Q2) How did you get to know about it, is there any story you want to share?

Answer: I was hyperactive and also going through episodes of severe depression which made me wonder why am I ecstatic at one moment and down the dumps in another moment. There was deviation in my sexual behavior which was a cause for worry and which made me guilt ridden. I goggled and got to know of an NGO that provides free counseling. The counselor recommended I must see a psychiatrist. I tried confiding in my parents however my father was not convinced and was reluctant to take me to a psychiatrist. I was a law student then interning with a senior lawyer in whom I had confided I had this problem. He knew my father, my father met him and he prevailed over my father. I need professional help and accordingly I was taken to a psychiatrist.

Q3) How long has it been?

Answer: I was diagnosed on the basis of a psychometric test by a clinical psychologist in 2004 and since then I have been under treatment and on medication. It's been nearly 16 years.

Q4) Are you on medication?

Answer: Yes I am on medication like mood stabilizers, Anti psychotics, Anti seizures, Antidepressants etc.

Q5) How is it affecting your life?

Answer: It has delayed my marriage. I wonder if I should marry or not. It has affected my stability and consistency at work. I have changed jobs. It has created interpersonal problems. It affected me academically. I took an additional number of years to obtain a law degree.

Q6) How is your work life?

Answer: In my current job and in the last 3 years or so I have managed well. I am a senior lawyer in a law firm and I am basically a freelancer. This assignment suits me very well.

Q7) What do you think that ordered people don't understand?

Answer: As far as ordered people are concerned on account of poor psychoeducation in our country they are prejudiced and have preconceived notions about mental illness. They are under the impression mood swings happen to normal people too but fail to understand that mood swings which a person living with bipolar suffer is different also far more severe and intense and as a result of neurochemical imbalance.

Q8) Do you want to convey any particular message to the ordered people?

Answer: Don't stigmatize people with mental illness. Mentally ill need empathy and not sympathy. Mental Illness is not insanity; it's merely a chemical imbalance in the brain for which treatment is available and people can live a productive life.

Q9) What do you think that psychology as a sector needs to develop?

Answer: The government has a key role in promoting psychology and psychology must be mandatorily made part of school and college curriculum to educate people. There is a need for awareness to be created.

Q10) Do you have any creative things that you have written and you want it to get published?

Answer: I have been an avid blogger and would love my blogs to be published. The links are as hereunder:-

One Poem:

My Poem on Lockdown:

> *Lockdown is a big mess*
>
> *Lockdown does not allow you to buy new dress*
>
> *Lockdown has caused tremendous boredom*
>
> *Lockdown hope does not take away permanently our freedom*
>
> *Lockdown is pretty uncertain*
>
> *Lockdown has made everyone get unnerved for certain*
>
> *Lockdown has tested our patience*
>
> *Lockdown has enhanced our faith towards God's reverence*
>
> *Lockdown has affected one and all*
>
> *Lockdown has spared*

none at all

Lockdown has been house arrest

Lockdown lifting should lead to peaceful rest

One Article: Radical Islam overshadowing liberal Islam

A peace loving individual who is civilized, sane and educated would abhor any kind of religious extremism and would be repelled by puritanical bigotry. Islam the last revealed religion has spread far and wide, There is a postulate its the fastest growing religion in the world. The media has always had a inbuilt bias against Muslims and it has projected Islam as a blood thirsty cult, however it can't be blamed for it as Muslim intellectuals have failed to oppose the hardliners in letter and spirit as they have held sway the clergy who have tremendous influence over Muslims have rarely trodden the path of modernism and always treated dissenters and rebels among Islam as apostates and condemned them with divine displeasure. Due to the misdeeds of a few black sheeps, the world has held an entire community at ransom.

Islam comes from the root word salaam which means peace, its five pillars encompass all virtues mankind can ever conjure and conceive.The prophet despite being unlettered was unparalleled in his wisdom and imparted a doctrine which is a gospel truth and of universal significance. Islam compares killing of one innocent with perpetrating a pogrom on mankind. In the Holy Quran backbiting and slandering is compared with eating dead meat of one's own brother and the Koran ordains moderation in eating and drinking, modesty in dressing, restrain in professional pursuits and steadfast abiding of principles in day to day living. Jihad is a duty cast on every Muslim to strive to become a better human and to please the almighty in the best possible manner, jihad has no implications of violence or is not synonymous with terrorism. When terrorists claim if they die in an act of terrorism they will be conferred with sensual pleasure with umpteen virgins in heavenly abode smacks of filthy mind, misled approach and murky consciousness, such miscreants need to be told do they consider their almighty so befallen that he is running a den of forbidden pleasure. On judgement day the almighty leaves no stone unturned in delivering a verdict on afterlife and terrorists without a doubt are doomed to the worst abodes of hell in which there is unmitigating miserable existence.

Understanding Islam is the need of the hour in the right context through people who understand it not just in context of intellectual niceties but also its metaphysical connotations. There is emphasis on dialogue in the Islamic scriptures with nonmuslims to project the article of Islamic faith in the right light to dispel myths and put misconceptions at rest. Muslims must endeavor to set a good example amidst a few who have gone astray to regain the glory of era when Muslim intellectuals ruled the roost. Muslims of today's day and age need conscientious spiritual mentors who don't fall prey to obscure orthodoxy and mindless conservatism at the altar of so called devout and pious religiosity

CHAPTER 5

Participant: *Mentally ill*
Age: *68years*
Gender: *Male*
City: *Mumbai*
Occupation: *Service, Full-Time*

Q1) What are you suffering from?

Answer: I am suffering from Bipolar Mood Disorder and also Pulmonary Embolism and Pulmonary Hypertension.

Q2) How did you get to know about it, is there any story you want to share?

Answer: When I was 23 years old, one night at 4 AM I suddenly woke up with a panic attack and negative thoughts racing in my mind. I was terrified and did not know what or why it was happening to me. As the day progressed the fear and panic reduced, but for the next 2 more nights at around 4 am I again woke up completely terrified and depressed and the mind full of negative thoughts and future-looking hopeless that I realized I was suffering from depression, as my mother also suffered from a mental illness at that time, and was under the treatment of a psychiatrist. I then told my father what had happened and he should take me to the same psychiatrist who was treating my mother. Initially, he did not believe me, but when I insisted he fixed an appointment for me and took me to the doctor.

Q3) How long has it been?

Answer: It has been 45 years since I first met the psychiatrist for this mental illness.

Q4) Are you on medication?

Answer: Yes, I am on medication continuously for the last 45 years taking them every day.

Q5) How is it affecting your life?

Answer: For the first 3 decades, medicines did not work for me. I would get bouts of depression with anxiety and panic attacks about 3 to 4 times a year, each lasting for 6 to 10 days. During these bouts my first psychiatrist would give me ECT's, 2nd would give me 5 to 6 injections a day for 5 days, and my 3rd psychiatrist would increase the dose of the prescribed medicines. My fourth psychiatrist who had just come out of medical college and to whom I was the first patient of BPAD, tried a trial and error method on me with a few medicines and was able to find out a cocktail of medication that was effective for me. This trial and error method took 2 years to complete, but all my BPD symptoms went into remission and for the last 10 years or so I am stable and living a normal life.

Q6) How is your work life?

Answer: My work life is good. I work for a partnership company and my mental illness is known to the owners of the company. They are sympathetic to me. My relationship with other staff members in my workplace is good as me being the oldest person in the company, can solve many of their difficulties.

Q7) What do you think that ordered people don't understand?

Answer: Ordinary people who do not have a mental illness just do not understand the concept of psychosis and particularly the paranoid thoughts a mentally ill person gets. This is because there is no logic behind it.

Q8) Do you want to convey any particular message to the ordered people?

Answer: Mental illness can be had by anybody, not necessarily it be hereditary but it can be had by others also and people should know that it is just like any other physical illness. Nowadays it can be very well managed by medical science and with proper cooperation of the other members of the household, this process becomes a little bit easier.

Q9) What do you think that psychology as a sector needs to develop?

Answer: It should be made cheaper and accessible to all.

Q10) Do you have any creative things that you have written and you want it to get published?

Answer: I have to date answered more than 2000 questions in the mental health section of Quora.

How do I console a family member?

First thing to remember is no matter what you should not lose your cool.

The one whom you're consoling is hurt, and doesn't show any signs of negative behavior.

Be there till they vent out. Don't force it out of them. Give them time and little personal space.

Be around them just so that they don't feel alone.

When they start expressing their thoughts, listen first then empathize.

They would usually start blaming what could've been done to change. Do not react to it. Just listen. Any attempt of fueling the fire may lead to the possibility of catastrophic events in future.

Stick to them as long as they start showing any concern to anybody besides themselves.

The above said works best depending on how close you're to them. If you're not, then my suggestion would be taking the responsibility of availing the closest kin.

Will helping others help me?

Yes. Well, only when helped to a certain limit. Not far beyond your capabilities.

I had always found joy in constantly helping someone out.

Needless to say, I always kept my materialistic desires to a minimal.

By helping someone, you'll find your life more meaningful than before.

You must have definitely come across the book named 'the monk who sold his Ferrari'.

I'm not certain about the whole story as I myself yet to read the book. But it does sound like finding joy in giving up your materialistic belongings to achieve something grateful.

Transcript of the Participant's conversation with Shivani Thapliyal

You can start from your first day:

Well, first day what happened was, one night suddenly i woke up at 4 o'clock you know with panic attack and lot of negative thoughts in the mind and i was terrified and i didn't know what was happening to me and i couldn't sleep, i was very very restless and somehow i waited till the sunlight was there and i thought it must be something i ate like food poisoning or something like that. Then slowly slowly as a day progressed I became ok and i didn't tell it to anybody but slowly it went away. It happened the next day also and it happened on the third day also. Three days, it happened continuously.

Nobody noticed?

Nobody noticed like that, my behavior was not bad. My behavior was sane but i was feeling very uncomfortable and a lot of negative thoughts were running in my mind and i was not feeling to do anything but i was feeling very panicking throughout the day. So, after the third or fourth day I told my father and mother, they said no nothing can happen to you, why are you getting afraid? So i said, no i couldn't sleep properly for three nights. So, they took me to my family doctor.

Family doctor? General Physician?

Ya, GP. Mbbs doctor. So my head was also paining and he then said it must be something to do with your eyes, you must have got spectacles, so he sent me to an optical vala, so i went to the optical shop to check my eyes. He said, my eyes are ok. So again we went to the general GP but this time i told him that there is nothing wrong with my eyes, i think something is wrong with my mind only. So what to do, I said you have to send me to a psychiatrist.

And this was happening at what age?

23. And that time my mother was already suffering from a mental illness, and she was been taken to a psychiatrist

Do you think that it can be genetic?

Ya of course it's genetic. I am sure about it. And then I went to the psychiatrist and he first asked me what is your name, what is your age, what do you do and where do you study and this and that and then he asked me to tell me your problem, so I told him that I am suffering from depression. So he started laughing and he said what is the meaning of depression? So, i gave him all the symptoms but i had more or less in my mind rehearsed it all that what to tell him when he will ask me. I am feeling dull and i am feeling lethargic and i am not feeling enthusiastic and i don't feel like eating and i don't like to listen to music and nothing seems to be good now.

So, what the doctor said?

Doctor said nothing, my father was there with me so he made me go out and then after sometime my father came out and he said come and let's go. He has given the prescription to my father, I remember the medicine that tablet called tofranil was given, it is a tricyclic antidepressant and valium tablet was given, valium is diazepam. So, father said tomorrow you have to come along with me to the doctor's clinic. I said ok. So I took the valium and tofranil and I slept, because of the tablet that day I got proper sleep and I didn't wake up at 4:30 in the morning. Then the next morning, early morning without eating anything and drinking anything, I went to the doctor's clinic. So my father said lie on the bed and then the doctor came and along with him anesthetic were also there. Lady anesthetic gave anesthesia and I lost my consciousness and then he gave me one ECT.

So they didn't take any consent from you for ECT?

No they didn't. My father's consent was my consent. Father was there.

But as an adult you also have some rights!

I was there but that time he must have taken into consideration that I am beyond taking consent. Those days chalta tha yeh sab! Puchne ki zarurat nahi tha! What is good for me, my father can make a decision yes or no. Then in 3 to 4 months i became ok but what happened is that the ECT, i forgot a lot of things and my short term memory also got bubbled up. I was a science student and that time i was an engineering student, all the formulas i forgot, all the calculus i forgot, all the organic chemistry i forgot. I was trying to read but couldn't remember also because of that. It was total amnesia. I just couldn't understand what to write, my mind became totally blank because of ECT. But the depression went away in 3 -4 months and that waking up at 4 o'clock went away and the fear, panic and all that went away. Then after six months I stopped the medicines.

I went and joined another college then, I gave up that education and I enrolled in a diploma course in textiles. After 2 years again I got the same feeling of depression.

How did your friends react that time?

My friend reacted in the same way, they used to come and meet me also, they used to take me out. I used to go along with them. My friends are very nice, the ones they were with me that time, are also friends in the present time. Right from school days, friends were there at that time, and are now also my friends.

So after two years, I again got a relapse. So, we went again to the same doctor. Again he said that you need ECT. So, again ECT was given. This went on with that doctor for about 10 years.

10years? And he never told you about what is happening?

Nothing.

So he was just doing the treatment, trial and error?

Yes.The doctor never spoke to me at all. When you go in he will give you 15 minutes of his time. He will ask you what is happening? What is this? How are you feeling? Then he will take a stethoscope and he will touch here, here, here and then he put it on my forehead. I don't know why he was putting the stethoscope on my forehead. Just to check your reaction. And then he will move his prescription paper and he used to write it. I was surprised that he didn't ask me any deep questions, he didn't allow me to talk in between, nothing. No questions, nothing. And the doctor was so famous that everytime he used to call us at 7 o'clock and take it in at 10:30am. He had a cabin in a big clinic and in the center there was a big sitting area, and the circumference of the round sitting area there were cabins of different doctors. One of the cabins he used to sit. And all the patients and their caregiver used to come and sit in the center and he used to go on calling one after the other and I used to see that people who came after me were called before me and I used to be called the last. After me he used to come out and go home. I don't know, maybe that was part of his treatment for me or i don't know. So, I used to believe that was the part of treatment for me. Come there at 7 o'clock and wait till 10:30 am and then go and meet him. And for these 3 hours, I have to sit in that room doing nothing. There were some old magazines kept there, so I can go through the old magazines. There was no AC at that time in the central area but there were fans but it was very hot and he had very good business at that time. If you want an appointment he will give the appointment after 2 months. He was a head of the department of a big municipal hospital.

But how he is dealing is not the right way?

It used to affect me and he made me alright. You forget everything, he used to make me alright. It's not like he did not make me alright, he used to make me alright but the thing is that i used to relapse. What can he do when I am relapsing?

Then in between what happened my sister's marriage came. And two months before the marriage I had an attack, a panic attack and depression attack. Actually it was a mania. So my father got scared, so this time one of my friends went and met that doctor because an appointment was not available. So he told him that you have to give him your appointment, because he has got his sister's marriage in two months and there is no time for it. So, he said, don't worry, in two months I will make him alright. So, because of that he gave me an early appointment and I went there and within one month he made me alright. In between two three times he made me admit also in some small hospital, it was a clinic.

Admit you for what?

Mania. He said this cannot be treated here he had to be admitted. So he made me admit one or two more places and there also the same thing they used to give me ECT.

How many ECT's have you taken?

14.

And every time you forget things?

Everytime i forget things. That is a side effect of that thing but there are no other side effects. ECT gives immediate results, ECT done and then you get the results, finish that is all immediately. It's not like medicine. I used to go to a professional college for textile engineering, and that time there was a management course also in Nirmala Niketan. Girls used to come for the course in Nirmala Niketan and we used to sit in the canteen on the fifth floor, both girls and boys and girls were very friendly with us. For textile engineering there were no girls, all boys but for textile management there used to be girls. We were very friendly with them and they were friendly with us. Once what happened he gave me ECT and then i came to the college and i was sitting there and some girl came to me and said hi, how are you? So my friend was sitting next to me, I just turned to him and said who is she? He said, arey you don't know who she is?

She said, what's wrong with him?" He said nothing, nothing, he is ok. Such things have happened to me. I completely forgot the face of people, that I know them, I completely forgot to recognize people, who they were. Anyway then i got fed up with this doctor, i said he is only an ECT master. So I said no, I have to change it. I have a cousin brother who has become a MBBS, so i asked him, so he said he has a classmate who is also a psychiatrist and he can recommend him to me. So he gave his reference. So I changed the doctor from ECT to this fellow. So this was a younger generation, the previous doctor was the head of the department. So, first of all he started giving me medicines, again I relapsed. So his method of treatment was injection therapy.

What was your age at that time?

About 33 -34 yrs. 10 years i gave the first doctor. So when I relapsed his treatment was an injection therapy, he used to give me 5-6 injections at a time in one day.

5-6 injections to treat mania and depression?

Yes.

And also he was giving you medicines?

Medicines are going on, in spite of the medicine I used to have relapse. Medicines toh band karne ka hi nahi hai, medicines toh chalu rehta hai. Medicines don't stop, in spite of the medicines I used to relapse. It happens to all of them, the relapse comes in spite of the medicine. So, he used to give me five injections: one in the right arm, one in the left arm, one in the intravenous in the left arm, one in the stomach of the right side and one in the left side, so many injections. So because of the fear of the injection only after 5-6 days, I used to become alright and he never used to tell me what type of injections they were. From his bag he used to remove a small veil and he put in the injection and he used to give me but he makes me alright in 5-6 days. He also made me admit 2-3 times.

For how many days?

4-5 days, when the mania was high. This injection thing again, i was with this doctor for 10 years, everytime i used to have this episode, every year 3-4 times i used to have this bouts. Sometimes he increases the medicines and controls it but if the bouts were longer and very high then he used to give me injections. So, I continued with him for 10-12 years. Then I thought, something is wrong, this is not the way doctor's are working. I tried to avoid ECT and then I landed into the worst of it that is injections. Now who is going to continue with injections, so i was talking to one of my friend's and his wife and his wife said that near our house only there is one lady psychiatrist, why don't you go there? She is a lady and she won't use any harsh method of treatment, try a lady one na, lady will be better for you and she is near your house also so the advantage is there. I said ok let me try, the first day my friend and I went there and met her. So she said, okay i have the time i will take you. She was also very busy, a lot of patients she had, now she has become old. She was the first one who introduced me to anticonvulsants. By the time lithium started on me, the first doctor started the lithium after 6 years, the first 6 years I wasn't given lithium because he thought it was only depression. After 6 years he came to know that this was bipolar and the second doctor gave me lithium only and lithium was not working. He should have given me any substitute for that but he never gave me anticonvulsant drugs that he never tried. This third doctor tried an anticonvulsant drug called zen retard and then the intensity of my bouts reduced. But it didn't stop completely, the intensity reduced. In those days I did so many overseas trips for my company, I became stable, a lot stable. I was still working in all these years, I never left my job. I was working but during this doctor's period, over the 10 years of the period i could do several foregin trips during that time, i was so stable at that time. But 100% i was not stable, i used to get 1-2 bouts per year. So, after about 10 years, that lady doctor had to go for holidays somewhere for one month, so what she did was, as a substitute she kept this another lady doctor, substitute in a clinic. And this new doctor was just passed out from some hospital as a psychiatrist and she didn't have any experience of working with patients. She was a very fresh doctor. I was just introduced to her when both of them were sitting and I went there and she introduced me and said that next time when will you come I won't be there but this doctor is going to look after you. I said i don't mind, if she can prescribe medicines to me i don't mind. So next time I went, what she did was, she cancelled all the medicines and she gave me a fresh list. I got a bit worried, I said doctor, do you know what you are doing?

And this was during what age?

This was at the age of 55 years. So I told her doctor do you know what you are doing? She said believe me Mr. I know what I am doing. You come and meet me after 7 days. And what she has done was there was a small amount of lithium and then there this zen retard and then there are 2-3 other medicines, all she removed. And she started me on divalproex and other new medicines. And she asked, have you taken this medicine before? I said no, I am taking it for the first, that's why I am asking you to do what you are doing. So she said, don't worry. And believe me I took that divalproex for the first day night and next day morning i woke up and i could feel the difference in my head that something has happened and it has happened for good. I could really feel the difference in my head that something has really changed for me, then next day again I took the medicine and again I was feeling a little better. Then after 7 days i went to her and i said that doctor you have done a good job. She said ya ya it's ok now we have to tune the medicines now, then she asked me some questions and this and that and then she added one medicine topiramate, one more medicine she added, then from there onwards she is fine tuning it add this, add that and then was doing it for the nearly next two years and ultimately we could arrive at the combination which stopped all my symptoms of mania and depression. There was slight fluctuation but they were manageable. Now from the last 10-12 years i am stable now because of this final doctor. What happened is in the meantime she got married and she went to the USA, so she stays in the USA and from there she comes to India for once in 2 months. When she is in the USA i can communicate with her on whatsapp or on gmail. I am using the same prescription from the last 6-7 years now, then there is no injection, no ect. It's just medicines.

Have you tried counselling also?

I went for counseling when I was with one of the doctors for one year. The problem was it was not a two way communication it was one way communication. I don't know what type of counseling it was. I used to tell my psychologist that you have to talk with me, it is not like that I have to talk to you. She said, no it is like that only, you can talk whatever comes in your mind but then i said then i can sit in my room and talk to the wall, then i don't need you. If that's the case then why are you required then? You have to talk in between, you have to challenge what i say, and maybe that time CBT and interpersonal therapies were not there or if they were not famous or not in use, i don't know. I did for one year but it didn't help me much and if it did help me I have an error in how it helped me.

It was more the medicines that helped you?

Yes, next day I could make out that there is some key that has opened. Another thing let me tell you what has helped me other than medicine. Medicine must have helped me 60% but 40% is something else. When I went to the lady doctor, she gave me 4 xerox papers of 10 cognitive discussions and she said you read it and learn it by heart. So she has given me the 4 pages of a 'feeling good' book. I can see in the bottom of the paper there was a book and the author's name. I came to know that this is a xerox copy of a book, so where I work there was a book shop, so I asked about the book they had , so I purchased the book only because what is the point of reading the 4 pages of the book. I should know the things before that and after that. So, I purchased the book immediately and started reading it. I got very very interested in that. So I read the whole book and I came to know the concept of cognitive behavior therapy. Then I started going to the book depo and started looking for books on depression, psychotherapy and all. I used to look for the names of the book in the newspaper or in the articles.

So you self educated yourself?

Yes, I educated myself. There was no internet that time, nothing was there. One day I took my books and showed it to the lady doctor. She said what will you do with this, give it to me? I will make it useful. So, I gave all the books to her. Now I also have a lot of books.

So you keep updating yourself?

Ya, and this knowledge that i have got is helping a lot you know because i am trying to understand what is happening with me and why it is happening with me and things like that. Because I am getting a rational feeling of what is happening to me, suppose some person is getting a panic attack, so if he knows what a panic attack is, he can easily take corrective actions. If he doesn't know what a panic attack is and he is suffering then he will be at a loss of words or actions he will just not understand what to do and he will be in a worse position than a person who knows what panic attack is. So knowledge in such cases is definitely a good factor for everybody to have. Everybody should know what mania is, what is going to happen, what happens in mania and how it progresses and what are the signs of mania. Then if you go on mania you can recognize it. Psycho knowledge is very important, if you don't have it then it's bad.

CHAPTER 6

Participant: *Mentally ill*
Age: *Mid 40's*
Gender: *Male*
City: *Vizag*
Occupation: *Salaried Employee*

Q1) What are you suffering from?

Answer: Diagnosed as Paranoid Schizophrenia.

Q2) How did you get to know about it, is there any story you want to share?

Answer: There were substantial changes in my responses to real-life issues in my personal, social, work life. I got concerned but was overwhelmed by the illness to actually put myself for treatment on my own. My well-wishers responded and I was taken to a professional for the start of diagnosis and treatment.

Q3) How long has it been?

Answer: From the onset of symptoms to get to a point to seek professional help, it was about 6-8 months. The diagnosis was done in a span of 5-10 days on admission to a supervised professional care institution.

Q4) Are you on medication?

Answer: Yes, the medication (medicines and dosage) now are very different from what they were during the worst phases. The medication is for life.

Q5) How is it affecting your life?

Answer: The illness or the medicines, effect of what on life. Both have had positive and negative effects on my life.

The nature of the illness is such that the established support system for a non-afflicted person does not suit well. A step-back on all fronts is required so that the illness can be bought to manageable levels. Like on the work front non-structured work could not be taken up i.e. fore-go of career growth. Work that causes irregular work-personal life timings cannot be taken up, hence the financial growth was stunted. In my case due to the severity, I had to live like a recluse multiple times causing large and frequent career breaks and loss of personal relationships. The flip side was that when I was down to manageable levels due to the medication, I got a deep sense of gratitude for my life, well-wishers. A new profound sense of life has developed through the fabric of life sustenance (Career, Personal/ Family, Social, Network, Finances) are lost forever. All medication has side-effects and life has to be managed with the medication and the side-effects.

Q6) How is your work life?

Answer: When now on medication with illness at manageable levels, I feel that I am as normal as any other person on getting the work done. As with any other person, I have my fair share of success/failures at work. Though the medication for life causes some extra levels of conscious effort to have a lesser stress work, my work is as good as any other person.

Q7) What do you think that ordered people don't understand?

Answer: There are multiple channels of information that non-afflicted (ordered) people resort to tell that mind-problems are just nothing, read some self-help book, join some anti-depression therapy, join some personality development program, do meditation. What they fail to understand is that these are techniques that help a person once the mind/thoughts in the mind are controllable/manageable. In the case of mental illness, the person loses sense of rationality/logical thinking which needs to be reinforced through medicines and a care-giving environment. Once the illness is at manageable levels the above suggested techniques can be used for personality growth.

Q8) Do you want to convey any particular message to the ordered people?

Answer: I have already stated what the non-afflicted people fail to understand above. In addition the labeling of an afflicted person as a person with diminished mental intelligence is wrong. Mental growth is fine in all us people only that due to illness it is not functioning properly. With medication and proper care, we are as good as any other person on using our intelligence.

Q9) What do you think that psychology as a sector needs to develop?

Answer: The outreach needs to be developed. In years gone by the channels for consultation were only in-person. Nowadays with technology multiple interaction channels are available and trained professionals in the areas of mind-illness-cure can use these to increase their outreach

Q10) Do you have any creative things that you have written and you want it to get published?

Answer: Did not understand the significance of this. I demonstrate a lot of creativity and original thought in my work-place scenarios. So not sure why creativity is to be restricted to something can be published.

CHAPTER 7

Participant: *Mentally ill*
Age: *40*
Gender: *Male*
City: *Mangalore*
Occupation: *Doctor*

Q1) What are you suffering from?

Answer: Bipolar affective disorder.

Q2) How did you get to know about it, is there any story you want to share?

Answer: I came to know after visiting a psychiatrist.

Q3) How long has it been?

Answer: 15 years.

Q4) Are you on medication?

Answer: Yes, I'm on medication.

Q5) How is it affecting your life?

Answer: After taking treatment life is not affected.

Q6) How is your work life?

Answer: Work life is good.

Q7) What do you think that ordered people don't understand?

Answer: They lack the understanding of symptoms and signs of most mental illness.

Q8) Do you want to convey any particular message to the ordered people?

Answer: They should treat mental ill people as normal people with love, affection and care.

Q9) What do you think that psychology as a sector needs to develop?

Answer: Public awareness of psychology.

Q10) Do you have any creative things that you have written and you want it to get published?

Answer: No.

CHAPTER 8

Participant: *Mentally ill*
Age: *28*
Gender: *Female*
City: *Allahabad*
Occupation: *Landscape Architect*

Q1) What are you suffering from?

Answer: Bipolar II.

Q2) How did you get to know about it, is there any story you want to share?

Answer: Diagnosed in Nov 2017.

Q3) How long has it been?

Answer: 3.5 years.

Q4) Are you on medication?

Answer: Yes I have been on single med for the past 3 yrs.

Q5) How is it affecting your life?

Answer: Every time I go into Mania I become more confused, but I become stronger every time.

I am still trying to manage my symptoms,

Thoughts were racing in my dreams at million miles a minute.

I woke up to the urge to call or tell someone to express myself.

I remember everything

Ups and down in weight

My brain is like water. I can learn any new thing.

My husband thinks i am deliberately making mistakes & there was fear of being kicked out.

Q6) How is your work life?

Answer: I know people with bipolar disorder are quite creative and passionate. Work life is good...my profession demands a high level of software skills, site visits and multitasking so...facing difficulty in memorizing many things at the same time. I hesitate because I hate change & are sometimes afraid of new technology or software. I can't take those days in office when I am going through my mania state.

Q7) What do you think that ordered people don't understand?

Answer: Ordered people don't understand our struggles and they want us to pretend like normal in front of other people. It's really difficult to pass those tough times with oscillating emotions.

Q8) Do you want to convey any particular message to the ordered people?

Answer:

Q9) What do you think that psychology as a sector needs to develop?

Answer: I feel like psychiatrists need to answer our questions... they should open up with us more if possible.

Q10) Do you have any creative things that you have written and you want it to get published?

Answer: No, when u feel exhausted after giving your best, you need to always remember you are alive for a reason. Don't plan to quit just because of the change of season.

CHAPTER 9

Participant: *Mentally ill*
Age: *28*
Gender: *Male*
City: *Yes*
Occupation: *Manufacturing Business*

Q1) What are you suffering from?

Answer: Bipolar Disorder.

Q2) How did you get to know about it, is there any story you want to share?

Answer: So apparently the Letter I wrote to me as requested by my psychiatrist seemed more "superficial" and "technical". So I am giving this another try with more "feelings" infused. Here it goes,

Dear Friend,

You were sitting in a class in your college, a friend came to you returning Rs 100, he borrowed from you. Co-incidentally the lecturer commented something on fake currency. Later you had to take an auto-rickshaw to the metro station and give the auto-driver the same note. I saw you terrified to the bone thinking that you would be "framed" in a fake currency case. It was probably December 2012. You didn't trust your friend or the auto-driver or anybody for that matter. You thought that you are under surveillance by the government and media groups. All your college friends, school friends, family, relatives were nothing but spies, trying to keep watch on you and contain you in any way they can. The whole world seemed to conspire against you. Everybody seemed to peek into your soul. You felt exposed. Mentally naked in front of everybody. That was your first paranoid experience.

You were scared to get out of your room. You sobbed hugging your mom and dad like a 4 year old. You felt terribly guilty for every lie you told them, for every time you overstepped your boundaries. You felt like you didn't deserve to live. You recited Hanuman Chalisa endlessly wondering if it could help. You even went through shamanic rituals where you were slightly beaten up, interrogated for having pre-marital sex or eating beef ? (I am a Hindu, so eating beef is a big sin for us). You were interrogated if you were possessed by some ancestor of yours or maybe a demon. It was torturous.

Finally you were being "framed" "mental" when your family took you to the psychiatrist somewhere in January 2013. You were shivering thinking that everybody is trying to put you away in a mental hospital where you would remain for the rest of your life. But it was just the psychiatrist. You were told you suffered a psychological shock which led to clinical depression. A few medicines were prescribed and that was it. Your friends inquired, at the behest of your parents, if you had taken any drugs. But you were on another high which led to this. A high of over-ambitiousness, over-confidence boosted by all the motivational material you were voraciously consuming. Motivational songs, quotes, videos, books all fueled what later came out to be known as mania.

Bipolar Disorder it was. Slipped into depression, you made a lame attempt at suicide. Drank 3 drops of Savlon and you realised, you weren't even capable of killing yourself. You felt like crying out loud at your helplessness. You did that. Crying and walking aimlessly 10 steps from one end to the other end of the drawing room with a humped back, trying to wear off the excess energy you thought you had which apparently was causing all the chaos in your mind.

A couple of months passed and you began to normalise. You gained 20 kgs, weighing over 100 kgs. Your mind seemed numb. You went back to college. Cleared your exams but missed your project. You joined a fitness group, lost 20 kgs, cleared exams and graduated, got a job. Your dosage was reduced to a bare minimum, to just one pill a day. You were in the best shape of your life. Your father suggested you stop taking the medicines. You did. And then you faced a terrible relapse. This time a higher dosage and with it all the weight gain. Since then i.e. August 2014, you were caught in a cycle of Weight Gain – > Heavy workouts to lose weight -> Panic attack after heavy exercise -> Paranoia -> Depression -> Higher dosage of medicine -> Weight Gain.

All this continued till 2019 April. Signs of hypomania appeared as a result of becoming over religious. Chanting mantras all day long. You became argumentative, aggressive, felt invincible, ready to burst out at people and even punch them. You were irritated to the core. You felt an itching sensation between your eyes on the forehead. You were terribly restless and irritable. You abused your colleagues and elders. You just wanted to "push back" in any way possible. You felt trapped and helpless. It was during this time that you realised you needed more help than usual.

I am glad you started paying attention to your psychiatrist, psychologist, joined a peer support group, enrolled in an online program which helped you see the brighter side of bipolar disorder. Most importantly you realised the importance of routine and a good social life in the treatment of bipolar disorder. It's good that you are trying to become a more disciplined and tolerant person.

It's great that treatment of bipolar disorder requires you to be a better person. Maybe it's not an "illness" it's just a wake call to become one.

Take good care of yourself. Keep your workout steady and keep following the daily routine you follow. Have a great life ahead!

Q3) How long has it been?

Answer: 7 Years.

Q4) Are you on medication?

Answer: Yes.

Q5) How is it affecting your life?

Answer: Weight gain. Laziness, fatigue. At times difficulty sleeping.

Q6) How is your work life?

Answer: My hypomania is disturbing my relationship with my business partners. Work feels overwhelming. I don't feel stable in a particular business.

Q7) What do you think that ordered people don't understand?

Answer: They don't understand the intensity of low and high moods.

Q8) Do you want to convey any particular message to the ordered people?

Answer: Be sensitive to a patient and don't dismiss their mental illness as weak mindedness. You have no idea how it feels like. Please sympathize, don't criticize.

Q9) What do you think that psychology as a sector needs to develop?

Answer: More psychologists, cheaper therapy. Collective promotional activities encouraging people to get help and see a psychologist, on a national level.

Q10) Do you have any creative things that you have written and you want it to get published?

Answer: I started blogging.

Ego, Anger and Relationships

You know the perfect recipe to ruin relationships is doubt, suspicion coupled with lack of communication and anger. Doubt and suspicion leading to trust issues. Trust issues leading to not being open about the problem with the person concerned, leading to irritation, anger and then a sudden burst of rage causing a disastrous confrontation.

If you value the relationship then such a confrontation will turn your world upside down. A conflict with your manager can cost you your job, with your spouse it can cost you your marriage, with a business partner or a major client it can cost you your whole business. Just a few moments of rage and your world will come crashing down. Relationships make you feel wanted in the world, in life in general. Life seems worthless if we cut loose our most valued relationships. It can lead to a terrible and suicidal depression.

Hence it is important for our mental wellbeing, we identify and preserve our most valued relationships. Some relationships need to be cut loose though. Certain ones drain us of energy and take a toll on our health and other valued relationships.

But the ones which we need to preserve, which we dearly value, need persistent effort of lowering down our ego. In relationships, conflicts are bound to happen. But what are these conflicts? A conflict of ideology, political, religious, social beliefs, self-image. When our core opinions and beliefs are challenged, when our self-image is challenged, it hurts and initiates a fight or flight response. Confrontation and avoidance is bound to happen in this case. Over a period of time it corrodes the relationship.

What if we don't form a self-image? There's nothing to hurt in that case. What is the need to label oneself as someone? Let society label you, but don't label yourself. Let society judge you but don't judge yourself. We had no identity when we were born. People started calling us by certain names, society put labels of religion, caste, economic status , occupation on us. We started identifying with these labels and formed our own opinions and ideologies. But it hurt every time there was a conflict. This was our EGO hurting. Why have a big ego then? Why an inflated self-image susceptible to damage?

Even if it hurts, getting angry will make the situation worst. Better to accept that you are wrong to save the relationship. What good is being right and letting your world shatter?

Such a perspective has helped me simplify my problems in life. I hope it helps you too.

Accepting Psychosis

I am having anti-psychotics, I do feel paranoid, but I never really accepted being psychotic. It's hard to let go of the belief that people are conspiring against you, because it feels so real. In psychosis you are convinced that your delusional beliefs are true.

Thank god I haven't had hallucinations. That would have aggravated the psychosis. Accepting psychosis gives you a new perspective to life. It allows you the flexibility of doubting your core beliefs.

"You need to work on your rigidity," said my psychologist. I said "what is the difference between rigidity and assertiveness?". She said rigidity is "My way or the highway" mentality. Accepting psychosis helps one realise that maybe "My way" is based on delusional assumptions which only "seem" very real at the moment.

I am now able to doubt every core belief of mine without being disturbed in the process. It does lower down your ego. Since now you can never be too sure about anything. Jumping to conclusions and being too judgemental is not an option now. It resolves the problem of mental rigidity and opens up your mind to new possibilities.

Approaching life with preconceived notions and rigid philosophies does not seem appropriate with this perspective. Accepting your weaknesses does open up new doors for you, I realised.

I am in peace now. My mind feels calmer. Maybe this is the ZEN approach to life. Knowing that what you know may not be true and you may know nothing instead. Maybe this is "emptying your cup". Approaching life with an "empty" mind. It is like being a kid again. Just observing things in amazement.

Having a calmer and richer life experience now and enjoying the bliss!

PEACE!

CHAPTER 10

Participant: *Caregiver*
Age: *60+*
Gender: *Male*
City: *Mumbai*
Occupation: *Part time employed*

Christian upbringing.

I am 60+ and my wife is 59.

Together we are caregivers to our D

We also have a son 30+ writer & media professional

Daughter's history:

She is 25 now.

Passed BA in Sociology

Currently not working

Started somewhere when she was 18/19 years. It was a low phase for us. I was into the business of Logistics services. Due to the economic downturn it gradually collapsed.. probably this and now the rift and differences with less money coming in affected all of us.

I could see she was without friends in her junior college, pursuing commerce, which actually didn't suit her. Took 2 years to clear her accounts and another subject.

Once when she was feeling low and breathless, we got her admitted to a hospital. The diagnosis should have been depression. But, the Doctor a MD known to us for several years treated her for the upper respiratory system.

After getting discharged, the depression signs were there and were getting more pronounced. We then took her to a well-known hypnotherapist. She took her fees, but could not do much. But, advised us to visit a psychiatrist at a government hospital for a better diagnosis.

They advised us on medication and did sort of counsel her.

We also consulted a counsellor Govt approved for slow learners and persons with learning disability. As her faculties had slowed down. She again, a Christian, advised us to go to a particular hypnotherapist instead of a psychiatrist.

We finally went to a psychiatrist along with her. She was angry and very upset with us for taking her there. Doctor's medicines' were given covertly, as she was in a denial mode.

She was in her first year of college – BA. The medicine had stabilization effects. We found her better and consulted this same doctor to continue or discontinue the medication. He advised, if she is better, then gradually over a period of 1 month the medications can be discontinued. Which we did. Parallel she was on homeopathy for some women related sickness along with this the depression medicines were given.

She then after her first year took up a vacation job. 15 days into the job, her delusions and hallucinations were back.

I did some search consulted a psychiatrist for proper medicines. We had to change at least 4 doctors till we found one in our local area.

She is more stable now, but on off our challenges continue – delusions and hallucinations.

As she is in denial mode, our main worry is we the caregivers will not be there with her always.

I and my wife will be happy, if she acknowledges her situation and acceptance sooner. She is also independent financially with a regular job. So, please help her.

She has also seen a proper clinical psychotherapist a few times. But, now she is not comfortable seeing him. Also to another counsellor she has been. The same story.

About Christians in general:

We are taught about God and the devil. Temptations and some bad habits could be devil's work. If someone has voices or delusions, then a spirit or multiple spirits have possessed the person.

There are Christian faith healers/exorcists who can banish the spirits.

Some of our people believe psychiatrist medicines can make the person more mad. They generally don't advocate professional help

CHAPTER 11

Participant: *Mentally ill*
Age: *34*
Gender: *Male*
City: *Mumbai*
Occupation: *Editor and Screenwriter*

Q1) What are you suffering from?

Answer: Body dysmorphic disorder and Attention Deficit Hyperactivity Disorder. I am not diagnosed with the latter but I am certain that you have it.

Q2) How did you get to know about it, is there any story you want to share?

Answer: I don't like taking pictures. I tend to obsess over my chin and teeth in the mirror. Sometimes, I think that I am Frankenstein's monster. I tend to get distracted easily, and have trouble focussing. As a child I was hyperactive and the people in my community would call me 'the little terror' as I used to run around like an energizer bunny on duracell batteries. Could never quite sit in one place. I am also very absent-minded and tend to misplace or forget things.

I have contemplated suicide many times and did even nearly succeed once.

Q3) How long has it been?

Answer: I learnt of BDD 2 years ago and ADHD recently.

Q4) Are you on medication?

Answer: No. I hate being on medication. It makes me feel like a zombie.

Q5) How is it affecting your life?

Answer: It has been sabotaging work and relationships.

Q6) How is your work life?

Answer: A little better as I pen movie scripts for a living. I still cannot handle tasks that involve editing as I tend to lose focus.

Q7) What do you think that ordered people don't understand?

Answer: Stating that it is all in the head does not help. I understand that this self perception is not necessarily logical. But I cannot help it. You need love and compassion.

Q8) Do you want to convey any particular message to the ordered people?

Answer: I have a successful career despite my problems. So much so, that companies withstand my tantrums. Genius does at times border on insanity. I am not implying that I am a genius. However, my IQ level is way higher than normal, and my reasoning skills are better than most people. Even the so-called normal people deceive themselves constantly.

Everyone is leading life based on what they think is right and true. However, what one deems as being right and true, are merely vague assumptions. At the end of the day, people may be leading their lives living under what is a delusion, isn't it?.

Q9) What do you think that psychology as a sector needs to develop?

Answer: Psychological tests are carried out on an arbitrary basis, generally. A battery of tests is usually not conducted, and a psychiatrist or psychologist delivers a verdict based on his or her judgement. Such an approach does not merit much in the way of trust.

Perhaps who are deemed to be normal suffer from an unknown affliction that is not on DSM. How do we know?

Q10) Do you have any creative things that you have written and you want it to get published

Answer:

The Missing Link for the Next Industrial Revolution:

The next industrial revolution

Security has been a major concern for disruptive technologies such as automation, robotics, 3D printing and the Internet of Things among others. The decentralized nature of the blockchain via its encrypted blocks could act as the perfect remedy to these security woes. Thereby, the blockchain could act as an enabling tool for the next industrial revolution, Privacy has fast become a relic of the past in the age of Facebook and Google. Advertisers, who meet a specific platform provider's criterion, have access to users' most intimate details, their habits and patterns for the purpose of elaborately tucked marketing algorithms. It's the price to be paid for living in an always connected world that has led to the monopolization of data and subsequent security offered being merely a farce.

Ostensibly, there is a need for a complete overhaul; promising innovations and ideas kept at bay have not come to fruition due to the overwhelming nature of security woes. A scenario where hackers take charge of a life changing innovation can quickly see it transform into something that is dire and life-threatening.

There is where the blockchain acts as a veritable panacea. The blockchain's ingenious design allows one to anonymously exchange information in a safe and secure manner, without the need for reliance on an intermediary like the government or a bank to keep things in check. Its self-regulating nature is what makes the blockchain a novel and paradigm shifting technology.

The next big thing?

The blockchain network is a lot like football, the playing field acts as the platform and when the nets register the goal, there is a thundering response from the crowd which acts the consensus. The only major difference being that the identity of the one who scored the goal and the goalkeeper would be anonymous.

Yet so far, we have merely scratched the surface of blockchain's potential. It is with the IoT that a significant part of blockchain's capabilities can be harnessed. According to data published by Grand View Research, the blockchain is expected to reach USD 7.59 billion by 2024, at a 37.2% CAGR.

Its unique capabilities allow it to be leveraged in various avant-garde technologies of the future like the Internet of Everything, Smart Defence, Automation and Fintech among others. Since these are connected technologies, without the blockchain, they are highly vulnerable to cyberattacks which are a pertinent point of concern for the near future. Ransomware and Denial of Service attacks are already very common. The blockchain remedies these problems due to its decentralized nature. The cryptography which is intrinsic to the blockchain allows agents to interact in a secure fashion and transfer assets across the globe at nearly minimal or zero transaction fees.

How it is going to help shape the industry?

The industry is undergoing a revolutionary change known as industry 4.0. This is where the steady consonance of various complementary technologies such as Automation, The Internet of Things and Artificial Intelligence shall bring about a drastic transformation in the very approach towards business and manufacturing.

The blockchain is the layer that shall consolidate the security of these platforms and enable them for mass adoption. For instance, with the aid of the blockchain, smart factories can autonomously order key engineering components, detect faults in the supply chain before their occurrence and streamline the manufacturing process to a much larger extent to cut down on lead times.

Smart factors shall usher in an utopia of truly globalized manufacturing while the adoption of key technologies shall help with optimization endeavours. Certain technologies like 3D printing will help reduce the complexity of the supply chain significantly. This would enable a greater market outreach and offer a boost to e-commerce

CHAPTER 12

Participant: *Mentally ill*
Age: *31*
Gender: *Male*
City: *Mumbai*
Occupation: *Entrepreneur (Fabric Manufacturing)*

Q1) What are you suffering from?

Answer: Type 2 Bipolar Disorder.

Q2) How did you get to know about it, is there any story you want to share?

Answer: I went into a full blown mania for almost 2 years, which finally led me to visit a doc, who finally diagnosed it as bipolar.

Q3) How long has it been?

Answer: Diagnosed 2.5 years ago.

Q4) Are you on medication?

Answer: Yes.

Q5) How is it affecting your life?

Answer: I am not able to live upto my full potential, I find it difficult to have conversation with my clients and suppliers, and the over networking aspect of my work gets affected.

Q6) How is your work life?

Answer: I could be doing much better, but due to support of my family and the fact that my father has his separate business in the same field helps a lot.

Q7) What do you think that ordered people don't understand?

Answer: I heard this line somewhere and it is exactly the right one... 'Normal people expect us to behave as if we don't have the mental illness'.

Q8) Do you want to convey any particular message to the ordered people?

Answer: The time that you want to leave us, is the time that you should specially stick around, because we aren't distancing just you, but also everyone around us.

Q9) What do you think that psychology as a sector needs to develop?

Answer: A strong awareness campaign.

Q10) Do you have any creative things that you have written and you want it to get published?

Answer: Yes and yes... But there is still time for that...I am currently working on an info-blog, it's still in its nascent phase but I am hoping to make it big. Also, I am working and then not working on a book, don't know if I will be able to finish it, but hoping so.

CHAPTER 13

Participant: *Mentally ill*
Age: *28*
Gender: *Female*
City: *Mumbai*
Occupation: *Art Educator/Artist*

Q1) What are you suffering from?

Answer: I am suffering from Bipolar Disorder.

Q2) How did you get to know about it, is there any story you want to share?

Answer: I was always a very quiet and shy kind of a child in school having various bouts of sadness, inferiority complex, problems in being social, no friends, relatives making fun and discriminating etc In 2012 when my body absolutely stopped functioning as in finding it difficult to carry out daily activities and crying 24/7 I was diagnosed with depression, was under severe medication and then in 2018 I was diagnosed with bipolar after asking my doctor firmly as to what is the problem.

Q3) How long has it been?

Answer: It's been since childhood but formally diagnosed in 2018.

Q4) Are you on medication?

Answer: Yes.

Q5) How is it affecting your life?

Answer: I can not describe how badly it has affected my life. Frankly I am still trying to figure out what aspects in my life are happening due to the illness. Some things that I have noticed are lack of focus, less productivity, anger, irritation, no friends, no social life and by that I truly mean it's zero, a lot of insecurity to the extent that I just feel that I should die before my caregiver I.e. my father because there is nobody else who understands my disease.

Q6) How is your work life?

Answer: Not very good. I have changed 5 careers. Even today when I am in the field which I am most passionate about, I don't feel like working, it takes a lot of self convincing to go out to take classes, I don't like changes too much but I have to deal with it as the profession is such.

Q7) What do you think that ordered people don't understand?

Answer: They can never understand the constant struggle because they feel such things can be dealt with easily with methods like meditation, yoga, and different courses offered by yog gurus like sadhguru and Sri Sri ravishankar. Also they don't empathise much because the problem is not visible.

Q8) Do you want to convey any particular message to the ordered people?

Answer: May god never give you or your loved ones any such illness because you cannot imagine what a person goes through, do learn to be more empathetic towards ppl, don't give them sympathy, just give them the same kind of help as you would to anyone going through any physical illness.

Q9) What do you think that psychology as a sector needs to develop?

Answer: Better psychologists. Their services are required when there is a problem or a trigger, not just once a week wherein you have to describe the whole week.

Q10) Do you have any creative things that you have written and you want it to get published?

Answer: I can give you pics of some of my art works. I have not written anything.

CHAPTER 14

Participant: *Mentally ill*
Age: *32*
Gender: *Male*
City: *Hyderabad*
Occupation: *Software Engineer (Frontend)*

Q1) What are you suffering from?

Answer: I was subsequently diagnosed with depression in the year 2017 and 2018, doctors said it is drug induced depression but I believe I have bipolar as well.

Q2) How did you get to know about it, is there any story you want to share?

Answer: Everything was fine until high school but as soon as I got into college my mental health started to degrade. I believe mostly because of the bullying from the people at my college. To get rid of it, I started to hangout with people doing drugs and alcohol just to feel belonged and feel protected from those who bullied me. It is then things started to get out of control. I started to bunk classes, had a long list of backlogs, disrespected my family and friends, harmed myself and even hated to live. Luckily, I completed the college in 4 years but the habits I developed during those 4 years took a toll on my health and career. It took me 10 years to get back to loving my life and people around me again. Though I still feel depressed from time to time, I am very proud that I am clean and sober now.

Q3) How long has it been?

Answer: The problems started in my 2nd year of college which was 2007 so probably 13years of suffering so far.

Q4) Are you on medication?

Answer: The doctors prescribed me anti-depressant, mood stabilizers, antipsychotic and sleeping pills. I used to take them but not anymore; not like I was facing any side effects, I was just being careless.

Q5) How is it affecting your life?

Answer: Right now things are getting back to normal but it has affected my health and career a lot. It's because of it I am now about 4-5 years behind especially in my career. Also, affected my relationships. I only had two romantic relationships so far and both of them ended up terribly.

Q6) How is your work life?

Answer: I have a history of job changes but now I enjoy what I do. Being raised in an engineering society I guess it molded me to like work that involves building things and it is what I am doing now.

Q7) What do you think that ordered people don't understand?

Answer: I know most of us think that people who don't have any sort of mental problems have some kind of stereotype against people like us but in my experience I have received criticisms even from all sorts of people. I think there are good people (who would treat everyone equally) and there are bad people (who would take advantage of conditions for anything) in both categories (ordered & unordered).

Q8) Do you want to convey any particular message to the ordered people?

Answer: Just be good to everyone. Same goes to the people with mental illnesses.

Q9) What do you think that psychology as a sector needs to develop?

Answer: Firstly, we should come out of this money making thinking. I have visited psychiatrists who are just there to rob their patients. They don't care about anyone but just themselves. Secondly, more people like Vijay Nallawal should come forward to break the stigma related to mental health topics. Once we are able to make it a social norm I believe wonders will happen.

Q10) Do you have any creative things that you have written and you want it to get published?

Answer: I used to write short poems when I was working in advertising but not anymore.

> *To whom do I belong?*
>
> *To the depth of briny blues*
>
> *Or to the warmth of golden globe*
>
> *To the mightiness of hilly highlands*
>
> *Or to the of enormous evergreen*
>
> *I belong to whosoever will have me!*

CHAPTER 15

Participant: *Mentally ill*
Age: *36*
Gender: *Male*
City: *Agra*
Occupation: *Operations Manager, Social Media Manager, Content Writer*

Q1) What are you suffering from?

Answer: Mood Disorder(Anxiety, Social Anxiety and Depression).

Q2) How did you get to know about it, is there any story you want to share?

Answer: 15 Years ago, diagnosed by a doctor.

Q3) How long has it been?

Answer: More than 15 years.

Q4) Are you on medication?

Answer: Yes.

Q5) How is it affecting your life?

Answer: Although, it has helped me a lot but sometimes makes me drowsy.

Q6) How is your work life?

Answer: Struggle with productivity and goal setting. Searching for satisfaction in my job.

Q7) What do you think that ordered people don't understand?

Answer: They don't understand that mental illness is like any other illness. Empathy and understanding is lacking.

Q8) Do you want to convey any particular message to the ordered people?

Answer: Try to be more empathetic and understanding.

Q9) What do you think that psychology as a sector needs to develop?

Answer: Psychologists should be more trained and be governed by an accredited organisation. There needs to be restrictions on bad practices.

Q10) Do you have any creative things that you have written and you want it to get published?

Answer:

My Story

I belong to a middle-class family from a 2 tier city of India. I had a happy childhood and had a great family. We lived in a combined family setup. The story of my fight with mental illness started 24 years ago when I was 12. I had just returned from evening games with my friends. I was in the kitchen with my Mom and Taiji(Aunt) enjoying the smell of tasty food they were cooking. But suddenly I fainted. One of our family helpers, Durga saved me from falling. While unconscious, I had an epileptic attack!!!

In my unconsciousness, I was going through epileptic fits. The nature of epileptic fits was such that you are 10 per cent conscious and 90% unconscious. In my case, it was a partial seizure. When I went through the fits, I was not able to control the left side of my body. The left side of my body went through multiple jerks. During the fits, my eyes were closed but I could partially see and feel the things around me sometimes. I remember my Taiji and my Mother shouting "Kya Hua?". The fits felt like paralysis where I had no control over myself. I had no control over things around me. After a bout of an epileptic fit, I became unconscious.

It was with the immediate response and help of my cousin and other family members that I was taken to a neurologist! The doctor immediately prescribed me with medicine to control my seizures. He also asked for an EEG test. It was diagnosed that I was epileptic with partial seizures. I was put on Tegretol.

After being put on medicines, my seizures were in control. The frequency of seizures decreased from once in a day to once in 15 days and subsequently once in a month. It eventually got to once in six months or once in a year. The medicines were heavy and made me slow. I was in the 6th grade back then and my marks dropped in the first and second term exams.

Before 6th grade, I was one of the best students in school but after being diagnosed with epilepsy, I struggled with my studies and daily life. I became more anxious as the fits took place in front of the whole family. I felt that there was something wrong with me. Although my parents were very supportive, they told me not to talk about this as I was alright and there was nothing serious. From my sixth grade up until now I have struggled through many of my academic pursuits.

My fits totally went away when I was in class 9th. I was off medicine after that. But there were other struggles waiting for me. I had become anxious. Somewhere in my mind, there was a feeling that I was not normal. Although, my parents were very supportive and always asserted that you are completely alright. During high school, I performed good and scored 75%.

When I was in 12th grade, my sister Neha became very ill. She was diagnosed with Hepatitis D, which is a rare and complicated disease. Within 15 days of her diagnosis, she died. After this incident, I gave my 12th and scored average. I had no idea about what to do with my life. But at that time, everyone was doing Engineering and everyone in my family wanted me to pursue Engineering. So, I was enrolled in an Engineering course with computer science as the main subject. My father decided to move to Saudi Arab for better opportunities. I and my mother were left alone in India with my immediate family.

I tried completing my engineering but failed thrice in my first year. I told my father, who was in Saudi Arabia that I would not be able to complete it. When my father returned from Saudi, I was giving one last shot at my Engineering. I was not able to do it. I became very sad and dull. Someone recommended my parents to take me to a psychologist.

I was diagnosed with depression. I must be 21 at that time. I was referred to a psychiatrist by the psychologist. The psychiatrist put me on meds. I started to feel better. Even my anxiousness was relieved. Meanwhile, my father had opened a coaching centre. I decided to teach English and Computer Science.

I had become so fed up with myself that I didn't want to pursue education anymore but my parents wanted me to complete my education. I enrolled myself in a diploma. I completed the diploma but my parents wanted me to complete graduation. I also realised that graduation was necessary. So I enrolled myself in Graduation and completed it. I was one of the toppers in college.

During this period I was in a relationship and was off medicine for a period of 1.5 years. But I had a breakup in my final year of Graduation. I was again in a depressed state and this time I had become more irritated and sometimes had no control over my anger and whatever I said. I was put on Valproic acid with an anti-anxiety drug by my psychiatrist. I became lethargic and drowsy.

Since then, I have worked with Infosys, completed my MBA and now working as Manager in an MNC. But I have become slow in performing and doing things. I joined a peer support group and am under therapy for the last five years. I have been told that my condition makes me slow. My psychiatrist told me (after much interrogation) that I have a mood disorder which has mixed symptoms of depression and anxiety. I was even put on antipsychotics for some time. My psychologist told me that my anxiety was a bigger problem. Depression part was comparatively low.

CHAPTER 16

Participant: *Caregiver*
Age: *42*
Gender: *Male*
City: *Livingston, NJ*
Occupation: *Software Consulting*

Q1) Who is in your family suffering from?

Answer: My brother.

Q2) How did you get to know about it, is there any story you want to share?

Answer: First recall of the episode goes back to 1997 when we were in Kanpur, UP and he was sent by our family for graduation studies to Delhi. He stayed with our Aunt (Mausi) for a year then with Uncle (Tauji) for a year and then stayed alone for last year. Episode that required psychiatric help was in his last year when he was putting up alone. The pressure of competition and family-comparison led him to struggle on passing graduation/BCom and his NIIT computer's diploma in '97. He was decided by his parents to move back to Kanpur. He joined his desired MBA (Finance) by distance learning in Kanpur Univ, but during the distance learning he could not manage to have a job and learning go on together. Post his MBA he took teaching as his career for several years, where he was been let go by multiple institutes over the due course of several years with obvious periods of no-job. While I (younger brother) went on to the US for a job, and got married in 2006, he got into family pressure to get married, which finally happened in 2008. He has been reading, studying and doing a lot of academics. Which has made his personality as I-know-all attitude. His wife / my bhabhi got accustomed in few (not so easy) years to accept the facts. She probably is the best thing happened in his life, not vice versa tho. They got blessed with a boy in Dec, 2009. Since his arrival the mood and air have changed. I went back to India in Oct 2010, and called up a full family in NCR. He managed to do few jobs in Noida, and when we moved into GGN house, he managed to work in a financial firm for almost 3years. He has been out of work since 2018 now. Bhabhi is doing a Librarian job for families well being and to have her own outlets.

Q3) How long has it been?

Answer: From 97, till 2011 it was a diagnosis of depression and escapism. In 2011 the doctors diagnosed it as bipolar.

Q4) Is s/he on medication?

Answer: Yes, Epilex Chrono (I may be wrong in name or spellings). It keeps him calm and sound.

Q5) How is it affecting your life?

Answer: As a caregiver, and younger brother, it affects our worries to family. Socially and mentally since it is part of life, me & my wife do not take it as a matter to get out of, or judge as a third party. We are part of it. My own kid is Autistic.

Q6) How is your work life?

Answer: Extremely busy and occupied. I'm in an IT consulting leadership job.

Q7) What do you know about the challenges they face?

Answer: Comparisons and social challenges, and not being able to perform on par - led him into this state. He is extreme introvert too - just that he is in the BP group, and has not participated in discussions.

Q8) Do you want to convey any particular message to the community?

Answer: Be compassionate with people that you know, and try to give time and space for people to perform. Be aware that they may not even perform, but become part of this long and tedious training of your loved ones.

Q9) What do you think that psychology as a sector needs to develop?

Answer: Bipolars lack friendship circles. A normal being gains a lot from friends' inputs. Psychologists should be friends to Bipolars rather than doctors or therapists. Family folks can't be friends, and cannot penetrate in the I-know-all sphere.

Q10) Do you have any creative things that s/he has written and you want it to get published?

Answer: Nothing tangible.

CHAPTER 17

Participant: *Mentally ill*
Age: *33*
Gender: *Male*
City: *Delhi*
Occupation: *Chartered Accountant*

Q1) What are you suffering from?

Answer: Bipolar Disorder.

Q2) How did you get to know about it, is there any story you want to share?

Answer: My parents had seen some symptoms of behavioral changes in me when I was pursuing My CA Course. One day I went to Mumbai without informing my parents with hardly Rs 2500 in my hand and I came back after 4 days. This incident makes my parents realize that there is some need for medical attention and at that time they asked me to take the help of a psychiatrist but I was denied that and finally they decided to meet the doctor without me and they elaborate all the story with symptoms to the doctor.

Q3) How long has it been?

Answer: More than 10 years.

Q4) Are you on medication?

Answer: Yes but now in quite less dosages and also I use to regularly do the exercise and physical work which help me to tackle this suffering quite easily.

Q5) How is it affecting your life?

Answer: I would say initially it affects my life when I was denial for this suffering and I took some wrong decision which ultimately affects my relation with some of my friends but if overall I say it effect positive to my life, once I accepted my suffering of BPD, it make me more strong to achieve my targets and to start live life happily by thinking only " If I can become chartered accountant with my this suffering, I need not to worry for any hurdles in my life in future and now i took my this suffering as my strength from past so many years by remembering my bad time during depression which I overcame.

Q6) How is your work life?

Answer: Answers to all these questions are almost the same, until I had not accepted my work life was also in balance but once I accepted BPD I took every challenge of my work as a normal task and completed it without any major hurdles.

Q7) What do you think that ordered people don't understand?

Answer: They don't understand the suffering which the child is living with and many times they blame for the things which he might do during his manic or depression phase which is out of his control.

Q8) Do you want to convey any particular message to the ordered people?

Answer: if the ordered people find that some different behavior in any of their known then doesn't judge them immediately and label them mental or something else rather find out the reason for change of the behavior of that person. Also there are necessities to bring awareness in the general public about the mental illness is some chemical imbalance in the human brain due to which people with disorders have to live their life.

Q9) What do you think that psychology as a sector needs to develop?

Answer: I can't comment much on that because I am not in touch with this.

Q10) Do you have any creative things that you have written and you want it to get published?

Answer: No not yet.

CHAPTER 18

Participant: *Mentally ill*
Age: *25*
Gender: *Male*
City: *Patna*
Occupation: *Unemployed*

Q1) What are you suffering from?

Answer: I am suffering from trigeminal neuralgia and depression.

Q2) How did you get to know about it, is there any story you want to share?

Answer: umm through MRI scan and clinical analysis.

Q3) How long has it been?

Answer: Around 2 years now.

Q4) Are you on medication?

Answer: Yes I am on medication.

Q5) How is it affecting your life?

Answer: I used to live in severe pain as its also called suicide disease. i can't be productive as most of my time goes into pain relief.

Q6) How is your work life?

Answer: Right now there is no work life.

Q7) What do you think that ordered people don't understand?

Answer: Yes they don't understand mental illness and those issues that they can't see.

Q8) Do you want to convey any particular message to the ordered people?

Q9) What do you think that psychology as a sector needs to develop?

Answer: Yes a lot.

Q10) Do you have any creative things that you have written and you want it to get published?

Answer: I am working on it !

CHAPTER 19

Participant: *Mentally ill*
Age: *38*
Gender: *Male*
City: *Bagalkot*
Occupation: *'Assistant Professor*

Q1) What are you suffering from?

Answer: Bipolar Disorder Type-2.

Q2) How did you get to know about it, is there any story you want to share?

Answer: By self introspection, observation done by well wishers and later examination/analysis carried out by medical professionals (for the first in the year 2007).

I vividly remember the earliest incident that happened with me in the year 1993 (when I was in 6th standard) . . . We had been to a family picnic/trip to Tuljapur (holy place, temple of our family deity Goddess Amba Bhavani).

During the tour, that lasted for about 3 days, I was more exuberant than normally expected. I witnessed an unusual high level of energy & enthusiasm.(an episode of Hypomania). And after returning to my native, for the next one week straight, I lost interest in all the activities around me. Back then, I carried out the activities either as a matter of obligation or as diversion from the disinterest that was bothering me in that particular week. (an episode of depression).

Quickly thereafter, although things seemed returning to normal, this episode left a lasting impression on me and now I can ascertain that this was the earliest mood-swing that I had experienced because of Bipolar. Later in life thereafter, symptoms became more obvious, complications developed as a consequence and today I am here, in my adulthood, living and dealing with it.

Q3) How long has it been ?

Answer: In my opinion, the initial symptoms started manifesting at the age of 12 . . . So till date (i.e.2020), it has been 26 years now.

Q4) Are you on medication?

Answer: Yes, but the quantity and strength of the medicines is much less now compared to the initial days (early years) of diagnosis. I am presently on Quetiapine (50mg) and Lorazepam(0.5mg).

Q5) How is it affecting your life?

Answer: The mood swings that appear because of the mental illness affect my usual routine at home, my performance at work place and my relationships in social circles. Yes, overcoming this challenge does require strenuous efforts on my part.

Additionally, the side effects of the medicines, although mild, needs to be tolerated.

Q6) How is your work life?

Answer: It is mediocre, in the sense that the limitations due to the mental Illness affects the professional work. Stability, Consistency, Productivity and Efficiency are usually difficult to achieve. By normal standards, you appear as an odd man out there in the group. As a consequence, I have been compelled to maintain a low profile in my professional life.

Q7) What do you think that ordered people don't understand?

Answer: There are certain things that ordered people don't understand about mental illness, like :

- they don't understand the fact that mental illnesses are as serious and hurting as the physical Illnesses.
- they don't understand that mental illnesses are different from the normal episodes of emotional imbalances that any humans usually undergo in their life.
- they don't understand that mental illnesses can become chronic and stay for life long.
- they don't understand that with proper medication, care and support, people with mental Illnesses can also get normal and contribute a lot to society.

Q8) Do you want to convey any particular message to the ordered people?

Answer: I request the ordered people to please understand the fact that caring for mental health is as important as caring for physical health, if not more so. And as such, illnesses related to mental health should neither be neglected nor be stigmatized.

The society needs a broad minded approach to accommodate the mentally ill people. Also the ordered people in different sectors like education, police, legal, medicine, corporate etc. should receive some basic training and awareness regarding mental health and related Illnesses. This can greatly help in connecting and amalgamating the mentally ill people with the mainstream.

Q9) What do you think that psychology as a sector needs to develop?

Answer:

- The first thing this sector can aim to do is to improve the doctor to patient ratio. As such, the strength of the staff in the Psychology sector needs to increase appreciably from what it is now.

- Different disciplines of medicine and therapy do offer promising results for easing down the mental illness. As such, focus should be on developing an 'integrated' and 'holistic' approach to dealing with mental illness, where things like counseling, diagnosis, medication and therapy can work in a more coordinated way to handle the sickness.

- The Psychology Sector can certainly employ the advancements in the field of science & technology to its advantage in developing tools that can then aim in making the diagnosis & related treatment less painful, more effective, more accessible and more affordable.

Q10) Do you have any creative things that you have written and you want it to get published?

Answer: Well there are a lot of ideas in my mind about creative writings . . . I am yet to systematically work on them, in order to transform them into meaningful compositions first and then give them a proper shape, so as to get them published. Maybe, I will do it in the near future.

CHAPTER 20

Participant: *Caregiver*
Age: *28*
Gender: *Male*
City: *Mumbai*
Occupation: *Engineer*

Q1) Who is in your family/friend suffering from?

Answer: Fiancee.

Q2) How did you get to know about it, is there any story you want to share?

Answer: She wasn't aware about mental illness (BPAD) & she thought it's kind of depression going through since 2017, Doctor suggested her medication will lifelong & even she informed me before our engagement that's she's under medication & even I thought everyone in world are consuming some kind of medicine for some sort of illness. I thought will take her better care & she might come out of depression soon with certain Meditation, Yoga, Ayurvedic treatment. During lockdown she requested me to buy medicine for her, she gave me prescription & I ordered online but they didn't supplied & then enquired many chemist near my home,But they denied & I thought why these medications are not available easily even with prescription.Then I googled about medication which was prescribed & I was shocked & tensed about her health & wellness, then I read about about medicine side effects & asked to share doctor case file. She was diagnosed with BPAD in 2017. She studied through a vernacular medium & her parents aren't educated so it was a bit difficult to approach & ask about her health. But she is truly a gem & I love her very much.

Q3) How long has it been?

Answer: Since 2017.

Q4) Is s/he on medication?

Answer: Yes.

Q5) How is it affecting your life?

Answer: I don't know how I'll handle situations if I found her in pain., I'm worried very much about her.

Q6) How is your work life?

Answer: Lack of concentration & continue thought & searching for cure.

Q7) What do you know about the challenges they face?

Answer: Decision making, Weakness, Soft hearted, Sensitive, Low Energy, Low appetite.

Q8) Do you want to convey any particular message to the community?

Answer: Finding alternative ways to cope & cure with BPAD because these medicines are making them more weak.

Q9) What do you think that psychology as a sector needs to develop?

Answer: Treatment is not an option, Develop cure & don't play with life for just money. We have always treated you as God, But don't let these trust break.

Q10) Do you have any creative things that s/he has written and you want it to get published?

Answer: She finds difficulty to concentrate & memories., I'm working on her hobby if she finds any interest.

CHAPTER 21

Participant: *Mentally ill*
Age: *32*
Gender: *Female*
City: *Alappuzha*
Occupation: *Guest Lecturer*

Q1) What are you suffering from?

Answer: Bipolar disorder 2.

Q2) How did you get to know about it, is there any story you want to share?

Answer: Got invoked at the age of 22 through some verbal fights and misunderstandings between classmates.Symptoms were there at the age of 18.But left diagnosed.

Q3) How long has it been?

Answer: 10 years.

Q4) Are you on medication?

Answer: Yes.

Q5) How is it affecting your life?

Answer: Life going smooth.

Q6) How is your work life?

Answer: No problems.We need supporting colleagues.That's it.

Q7) What do you think that ordered people don't understand?

Answer: They won't understand the struggles we are going through.Makes random comments.

Q8) Do you want to convey any particular message to the ordered people?

Answer: They should be educated about the illness first rather than making comments.

Q9) What do you think that psychology as a sector needs to develop?

Answer: They should give proper psychoeducation to the patients as well as their family.

Q10) Do you have any creative things that you have written and you want it to get published?

Answer: No.

CHAPTER 22

Participant: *Mentally ill*
Age: *44*
Gender: *Male*
City: *Palakkad*
Occupation: *University Assistant*

Q1) What are you suffering from?

Answer: Bipolar disorder.

Q2) How did you get to know about it, is there any story you want to share?

Answer: Psychology magazine and psychologist.

Q3) How long has it been?

Answer: 20 years.

Q4) Are you on medication?

Answer: Yes.

Q5) How is it affecting your life?

Answer: Wrong decisions.

Q6) How is your work life?

Answer: Average.

Q7) What do you think that ordered people don't understand?

Answer: I'm not antisocial.

Q8) Do you want to convey any particular message to the ordered people?

Answer: Aware about their own stigma.

Q9) What do you think that psychology as a sector needs to develop?

Answer: Psychoeducation is a necessity for controlling symptoms and avoiding dangers in life. Psychoeducation is possible through many ways in this information era.

Q10) Do you have any creative things that you have written and you want it to get published?

Answer: I published a book 12 yrs back.

CHAPTER 23

Participant: *Mentally ill*
Age: *35*
Gender: *Male*
City: *Surat*
Occupation: *Government Servant*

Q1) What are you suffering from?

Answer: Anxiety Disorder.

Q2) How did you get to know about it, is there any story you want to share?

Answer: My sexual life in marriage was not upto the mark hence I approached a psychologist, to improve on that front, who after 6-7 sessions referred me to a psychiatrist who diagnosed me with Anxiety Disorder. The anxiety includes performance anxiety and hence unable to maintain good sexual relations with wife.

Q3) How long has it been?

Answer: One year.

Q4) Are you on medication?

Answer: Yes.

Q5) How is it affecting your life?

Answer: I'm unable to maintain a good sexual relation with my wife, which is lowering my self-esteem.

Q6) How is your work life?

Answer: It's good. I love my work. Sometimes I have temperament issues but mostly it's fine.

Q7) What do you think that ordered people don't understand?

Answer: None of us is perfectly ordered, in my personal opinion. Since everyone has their own peculiar disorders they, at times, are unable to appreciate others disorders.

Q8) Do you want to convey any particular message to the ordered people?

Answer: Please approciate the disorders in other people even if you may not have the one.

Q9) What do you think that psychology as a sector needs to develop?

Answer: People should stop using words like mental illness or psychosis or mental disorder and shall rather use softer words such as behavioural issues.

Q10) Do you have any creative things that you have written and you want it to get published?

Answer: No.

CHAPTER 24

Participant: *Mentally ill*
Age: *31*
Gender: *Male*
City: *Allahabad*
Occupation: *Family Business*

Q1) What are you suffering from?

Answer: Bipolar Disorder.

Q2) How did you get to know about it, is there any story you want to share?

Answer: A counsellor in Delhi told me about it after me telling my story that 6 months I was too motivated , extroverted ,sincere in work and active and 6months I'm depressed, lazy, lethargic, insincere and introverted.

Q3) How long has it been?

Answer: Approximately 10 years.

Q4) Are you on medication?

Answer: Yes, homeopathy.

Q5) How is it affecting your life?

Answer: Not much.'

Q6) How is your work life?

Answer: Too disturbed a lot of bad decisions regarding expansion has been done in my active phase in anticipation of better future without proper planning and homework as I feel that I can do anything, secondly in the depression phase I dont properly go to office only, don't talk to clients regularly which I should neither do I check the works which I should,which has lead to lot of losses in business.

Q7) What do you think that ordered people don't understand?

Answer: Most of the people don't understand this as they can't feel this and especially in India as there is very less awareness about BP.

Q8) Do you want to convey any particular message to the ordered people?

Answer: Treat the BP politely and if possible support him/her to get him a routine especially in depression as it's the most important thing I felt,secondly in manic phase if a BP says shouts at u without a reason or in a very small situation, plz ignore it and understand that he/she is not speaking so because he feels its,its just his phase !!

Q9) What do you think that psychology as a sector needs to develop?

Answer: Definitely yes as the awareness is very less in india.

Q10) Do you have any creative things that you have written and you want it to get published?

Answer: Not yet.

CHAPTER 25

Participant: *Caregiver*
Age: *70 years*
Gender: *Male*
City: *Thane*
Occupation: *Consultant*

Q1) Who is in your family/friend suffering from ?

Answer: My son, 37 year old, never married, is suffering from MH. I am his father as a caregiver.

Q2) How did you get to know about it, is there any story you want to share?

Answer: There is a long story since 2000.Briefly his lifestyle and behavior change.

Q3) How long has it been?

Answer: The clinical part known since 2004.

Q4) Is s/he on medication?

Answer: Yes.

Q5) How is it affecting your life?

Answer: Disruption, uncertain, unstable family, worried for future of son , wife health issues, financial huge breakdown.

Q6) How is your work life?

Answer: Retired from work in 2009. Always struggling for living and taking care of family. Huge loans.

Q7) What do you know about the challenges s/he faces?

Answer: He has no total control in mainly mental space . Since he has MI , even if he wishes to live a normal life, the willingness to accept his illness is missing. And his introverted personality is the main hurdle in his recovery.

Q8) Do you want to convey any particular message to the community?

Answer: Caregivers role is the most critical . We can be change agents in MH. What worked for me was, I realised myself in depth and supported him with no grudges, blame game..His life was more important than mine.

Q9) What do you think that psychology as a sector needs to develop?

Answer: The medical support people are not playing a full out role in MI. What is missing is dealing with MH patients with empathy.

Q10) Do you have any creative things that s/he has written and you want it to get published?

Answer: No.

CHAPTER 26

Participant: *Mentally ill*
Age: *20*
Gender: *Female*
City: *Firozabad*
Occupation: *Student*

Q1) What are you suffering from?

Answer: Cyclothymia.

Q2) How did you get to know about it, is there any story you want to share?

Answer: I was diagnosed with depression when I was 17 . Straight A student could barely read when turned 16, took almost a year to realise I needed help. The depression treatment wasn't working so hypomania was diagnosed then.

Q3) How long has it been?

Answer: Almost 4 years of cyclothymia.

Q4) Are you on medication?

Answer: I was on several medicines but now it's just lithium twice a day. Recently I quit my antidepressants.

Q5) How is it affecting your life?

Answer: I was lethargic so I stopped studying and was in my room for 1 year and was coping with new medicines after every few months but then it all was worth it.

Up and downs

Rapid cycles

Pretty much missed on my late teenage.

Q6) How is your work life?

Answer: I don't work yet but I am lagging behind in my studies.

Q7) What do you think that ordered people don't understand?

Answer: Ordered people need to know this is real. We need to educate us and them as well.

We suffer from the illness then suffer from their ignorance and narrow minded less.

Q8) Do you want to convey any particular message to the ordered people?

Answer: Please educate yourself regarding mental health. We don't need prejudice against us. We already are struggling enough.

Q9) What do you think that psychology as a sector needs to develop?

Answer: As I mentioned, we need to eradicate the stigma first.

Mandatory psychology classes in high school. In India nobody talks about it, I was 16 I had no clue what mental illness felt like and the internet made it worse. I am not the only person who struggled with mental illness, and there are many folks like me who need help and have no one to talk to. We need an environment where we can talk about it while being stigmatized and have a stronger support system while sailing the rocky stream.

Q10) Do you have any creative things that you have written and you want it to get published?

Answer: I write and have few short poems. So yes !

She jumped into the sky

It looked shallow

Little did she realize

The sky is hollow

She knew she was off track

She howled for a fellow

She lost it when

No one heard the bellow

Why it was still dark?

As after the blues comes the yellow

It felt all new and inspiring

Swimming in the sky in her mellow!

CHAPTER 27

Participant: *Mentally ill*
Age: *54 years*
Gender: *Male*
City: *Nasik*
Occupation: *Business*

Q1) What are you suffering from?

Answer: Bipolar Disorder/Mood Disorder.

Q2) How did you get to know about it, is there any story you want to share?

Answer: I had my first breakdown 15Yr back around 2005 but not treated for BPAD, had my 2nd episode in around 2010.

Subsequent minor episodes n finally in 2016 major depressive episode with 18months break from business activity & treated as BPAD.

During this period Explored, Reading, n Gained knowledge about BPAD & other co morbid challenges.

Rebooted my Business activity again in 2018 & continuing.

Best part of BPAD is it doesn't take away your Skills' and Capabilities.

Q3) How long has it been?

Answer: Can be considered It is associated with me since childhood but surfaced 15Yr back & treated as BAPD since the last five years.

Q4) Are you on medication?

Answer: Yes I am on Medication its part of life but trying to reduce dependence.

Q5) How is it affecting your life?

Answer: Yes it's challenging across all domains of life Personal, Emotional, Social, Family & Business.

Q6) How is your work life?

Answer: Am able to manage without affecting irrecoverable.

Q7) What do you think that ordered people don't understand?

Answer: Privileged people to remain in Denial condition (They think there is nothing called MI).

Q8) Do you want to convey any particular message to the ordered people?

Answer: Knowledge, Awareness & Acceptance will help them to Look at it in a more Holistic way, that will help them in long run as (Affected), Caregiver or Simply Human Beings.

Q9) What do you think that psychology as a sector needs to develop?

Answer: Psychology as a Sector has tremendous scope as profession & commercial potential.

I am Fortunate to have came across more people who are gone through this kind of life challenges (Not necessarily MI) overcame it & Freelancing in this field as payback to society. As a overall experience they are more effective.

Q10) Do you have any creative things that you have written and you want it to get published?

Answer: Not Yet done anything as Structured writing.

CHAPTER 28

Participant: *Mentally ill*
Age: *31years*
Gender: *Female*
City: *New Delhi*
Occupation: *Brand Consultant*

Q1) What are you suffering from?

Answer: Bipolar Type 1 and Borderline Personality Disorder.

Q2) How did you get to know about it, is there any story you want to share?

Answer: As a child and young adult, I struggled with intense anxiety, OCD, irrational fears and had difficulty controlling my emotions and maintaining relationships. As a young professional, with stress mounting, my mental health started to suffer even more. There was very little family support available to help sail through these difficult times. I had a few panic attacks that went addressed. In 2018, I had another nervous breakdown which led my friends to take me to Vimhans. There I was diagnosed by the attending psychiatrist and started my treatment.

Q3) How long has it been?

Answer: Close to two years now.

Q4) Are you on medication?

Answer: I have been prescribed Lithium for my Bipolar.

Q5) How is it affecting your life?

Answer: It has always affected my life, even before diagnosis. Emotional regulation is a big challenge since the intensity of my emotions is unrelatable by neurotypicals. It affects my life when people know and use that to take advantage of my vulnerabilities to their benefit, like at work. If people don't know, they find it difficult to relate with you or empathise. Half information and taboo on mental health conversations leads people to pretend like they care and try to accommodate but the burden is always on me.

Q6) How is your work life?

Answer: It's good. it could be better if I didn't have to put in more effort to manage tedious emotions or go through depressive phases that affect my productivity. It would also be nice to be in an environment where environmental support and well-being services were part of the deal. That's just a dream though. People think it's normal to be hostile or passive-aggressive instead of empathetic because who has the time to care. What they don't realize that the consequences of this for someone dealing with mental health conditions can be very disastrous and demotivating, pushing many towards suicide as well. There is obviously fear of discrimination that prevents this from changing any time soon.

Q7) What do you think that ordered people don't understand?

Answer: A lot. This requires a list that I am happy to take the effort to make:

- They have no real respect for the struggle and self-work it takes to heal from mental illnesses. It's a lifelong battle but they really wish they didn't have to deal with 'us'

- They think that they do not need to understand the conditions that surround them - whether it be anxiety or bipolar. For them, the problem is not theirs - but they don't realize that they are part of the problem because their responses can either help heal or drive the person further into misery

- They make little or no effort to adjust their own behaviours to accommodate someone who has a genuine inability to adapt their behaviours. They feel pity instead of empathy and only understand when it is conducive to.

- They gossip, spread misinformation, paint mental health patients in a bad light and make it appear that they are less than capable. Frankly, I feel they are just uncomfortable because they don't want to make an effort to learn and correct myths and misconceptions.

- They don't understand neurodiversity - the fact that everyone's brain is different, their early childhood experiences and backgrounds are different which leads to such issues, to begin with. They believe that they are better than the rest when frankly they are just conventional and possibly undiagnosed themselves.

Q8) Do you want to convey any particular message to the ordered people?

Answer: Someday god forbid, your family member, friend, child, sibling or parent could go through something traumatic and end up feeling less than 'normal'. If you do not have it in you to learn about their struggles and understand how to support them - you should work on yourself first because you lack basic compassion for another human being.

Q9) What do you think that psychology as a sector needs to develop?

Answer: Curriculum and educational programs that intervene at school levels so young students can grow up keeping in mind that their peers, and people in the future they meet could need them to have developed people skills that did not discriminate on the basis of these labels.

CHAPTER 29

Participant: *Mentally ill*
Age: *29*
Gender: *Female*
City: *Thane*
Occupation: *HR Recruiter*

Q1) What are you suffering from?

Answer: I am suffering from bipolar disorder 2.

Q2) How did you get to know about it, is there any story you want to share ?

Answer: I was in my 2nd year of college, around 2014 year it was.I was unable to write anything during examination and also change in my behaviour.

I along with my mother went to check up on our family doctor who diagnosed bipolar disorder.

Q3) How long has it been?

Answer: It's around 6 years I have been suffering from bipolar disorder 2.

Q4) Are you on medication?

Answer: Yes , daily i take around 3 tablets at night.

Q5) How is it affecting your life?

Answer: Earlier years used to affect me a lot. racing thoughts, less sleep , more shopping , talkative nature etc. But now after a few years it's not affecting much. I have more sleep and sometimes headache.

Q6) How is your work life?

Answer: Earlier work life was very difficult . I used to do a job for a few months then leave it. sometimes unable to go to the office for a few days. Currently it is not affecting much, as I started working as a HR recruiter job which is work from home. So I am able to perform well.

Q7) What do you think that ordered people don't understand?

Answer: Ordered people don't understand much of what all mental illness people go through everyday. They don't listen to what the person is going through and sometimes taking it causally.

Q8) Do you want to convey any particular message to the ordered people?

Answer: Ordered people should listen to a person who has mental illness and understand them. Assure that they are always there to help. Don't expect too much from them.Be there whenever needed.

Q9) What do you think that psychology as a sector needs to develop?

Answer: They need to develop like there must be compulsory counselling after doctor visits mostly to patients and caretakers also. At reasonable cost.

Q10) Do you have any creative things that you have written and you want it to get published?

Answer: I have written a story about my struggle with bipolar disorder. I would to share few parts of it

There I start my story which happened around 7 years back. It's my own struggle which still continues. So around 7 years back I was in college 2nd year studying banking and insurance. I was average in studies and that time more interested in acting and drama groups. Slowly my interest declined in acting too and started sitting alone, much depressed. Started neglecting studies, rather couldn't study much. Something was wrong but even me, my family and friends were unable to figure out.

Then my exams started, it was the worst day ever in my life, I was unable to write a single word, I remember vividly I wrote some story and almost started crying. Still that day brought tears in my eyes. At home also everyone notices my weird behaviour . I was helpless at that time, I couldn't understand what's going on.

My mother and sister took me to our family doctor. And there it all started, I was diagnosed with bipolar disorder. Forever the first time I got to know that word, never in my dreams thought I would suffer from such serious mental disorder.

For everyone at home it was a shock, I just couldn't understand what's going on, how to help me out, will I get cured? Many unanswered questions. So the same day I was taken to psychiatrist. Sitting there I was unaware what's going on. He diagnosed me with bipolar disorder. He didn't explain much, prescribe some medications. So then we google about bipolar disorder all about.

CHAPTER 30

Participant: *Caregiver*
Age: *33 years*
Gender: *Female*
City: *Gurgaon*

Occupation: *HR Manager*

Q1) Who is in your family/friend suffering from?

Answer: Mother. She is suffering from schizophrenia.

Q2) How did you get to know about it, is there any story you want to share?

Answer: I got to know from my father in my childhood.

Q3) How long has it been?

Answer: More than 20 years.

Q4) Is s/he on medication?

Answer: Yes.

Q5) How is it affecting your life?

Answer: A lot.

Q6) How is your work life?

Answer: Ok types.

Q7) What do you know about the challenges s/he faces?

Answer: How she can accept her disease.

Q8) Do you want to convey any particular message to the community?

Answer: Yes please reduce the price of the injection as it is very costly. Monthly cost is 10 k.

Q9) What do you think that psychology as a sector needs to develop?

Answer: Creating a medicine which should have an effect on the patient so that the patient should accept their disease.

Q10) Do you have any creative things that s/he has written and you want it to get published?

Answer: No.

CHAPTER 31

Participant: *Mentally ill*
Age: *40*
Gender: *Female*
City: *Delhi*
Occupation: *Unemployed*

Q1) What are you suffering from?

Answer: Bipolar.

Q2) How did you get to know about it, is there any story you want to share?

Answer: Nope.

Q3) Are you on medication?

Answer: Yes

Q4) How long has it been?

Answer: 5 years.

Q5) How is it affecting your life?

Answer: It affects my day to day living.

Q6) How is your work life?

Answer: Quit my job.

Q7) What do you think that ordered people don't understand?

Answer: That people with mental illness are normal people with hopes and desires.

Q8) Do you want to convey any particular message to the ordered people?

Answer: Treat them with dignity and respect.

Q9) What do you think that psychology as a sector needs to develop?

Answer: We need more mental healthcare professionals in India.

Q10) Do you have any creative things that you have written and you want it to get published?

Answer: None.

CHAPTER 32

Participant: *Mentally ill*
Age: *31*
Gender: *Male*
City: *Bangalore*
Occupation: *Aerospace Engineer*

Q1) What are you suffering from?

Answer: Bipolar disorder.

Q2) How did you get to know about it, is there any story you want to share?

Answer: It was diagnosed very late after 9 years. It started when I turned 18 and entered college. At age 26, it was diagnosed. Now I am 31 and learning to manage the disorder.

Q3) Are you on medication?

Answer: Yes.

Q4) How is it affecting your life?

Answer: It brings lots of ups and downs in life. It is defining who I am and leading to disciplined life. It affects spiritually, emotionally as well.

Functionally I am leading a good life but my life would have been much better progresses without it.

Q5) How is your work life?

Answer: It gets challenging at times. It is ok but becomes difficult to set goals.

Q6) What do you think that ordered people don't understand?

Answer: They can't empathise. Even they dont give sympathy too.

Q7) Do you want to convey any particular message to the ordered people ?

Answer: No. Better to build awareness for them.

Q8) What do you think that psychology as a sector needs to develop?

Answer: It needs to develop as all of the people can benefit from them.

Q9) Do you have any creative things that you have written and you want it to get published?

Answer: No but I would like to get it done in future.

CHAPTER 33

Participant: *Mentally ill*
Age: *23 years*
Gender: *Male*
City: *Ghaziabad*
Occupation: *Student*

Q1) What are you suffering from?

Answer: Bipolar Disorder.

Q2) How did you get to know about it, is there any story you want to share?

Answer: When I got my manic attack.

Q3) How long has it been?

Answer: 5 months.

Q4) Are you on medication?

Answer: Yes.

Q5) How is it affecting your life?

Answer: Unable to focus on studies.

Q6) How is your work life?

Answer: I study and do not work.

Q7) What do you think that ordered people don't understand?

Answer: They often do not understand.

Q8) Do you want to convey any particular message to the ordered people?

Answer: No.

Q9) What do you think that psychology as a sector needs to develop?

Answer: Yes, it needs to develop.

Q10) Do you have any creative things that you have written and you want it to get published?

Answer: No.

CHAPTER 34

Participant: *Mentally ill*
Age: *23*
Gender: *Male*
City: *Jamshedpur*
Occupation: *Student*

Q1) What are you suffering from?

Answer: Bipolar Disorder.

Q2) How did you get to know about it, is there any story you want to share?

Answer: I was 19 and was studying in an engineering college when I experienced my first manic episode. Then my father took me to a psychiatrist and the doctor diagnosed me with bipolar disorder.

Q3) How long has it been?

Answer: I was first diagnosed in 2016.

Q4) Are you on medication?

Answer: Yes.

Q5) How is it affecting your life?

Answer: It's running my life. I was a good student previously but now i am useless. I lost all my confidence and all i think now is to commit suicide. I once attempted suicide but bad luck, i survived. After that there was a lot of family drama and so i didn't attempted suicide again. But these days i often think about committing suicide. I can't concentrate, I can't focus, i lost all my interest in life and household work.

Q6) How is your work life?

Answer: I am a student, so no work.

Q7) What do you think that ordered people don't understand?

Answer: They don't understand my pain. They don't understand why i am lazy. They don't understand why I sleep so much. They don't understand why I procrastinate so much. They make fun of my illness. They don't understand why i can't focus and concentrate.\

Q8) Do you want to convey any particular message to the ordered people?

Answer: We mentally ill people don't do much productive work according to you but we try to do our best. We may be sitting idle but we are in pain. Try to understand it.

Q9) What do you think that psychology as a sector needs to develop?

Answer: I don't know about psychology but i would request all the mental health professionals, please try to be more sensitive towards the patients. They are also human and are in pain. They are not your client but a person who came for help. And therapies and medicines should be cheaper.

Q10) Do you have any creative things that you have written and you want it to get published?

Answer:

ज़िन्दगी की शाम अब आने को है।

महफ़िलो में जाम अब आने को है।

बीती बातें भूल जाऊं कैसे मैं।

मेरा वो इन्तेक़ाम अब आने को है।

उम्मीदे हैं बेइंतहां खुदसे।

अरमानो का अंजाम अब आने को है।

कशमकश से बीत गयी यह जिंदगी।

तकलीफो में आराम अब आने को है।

बहुत खेल लिया अपने अखशो से हमने।

सपनो का मकाम अब आने को है।

CHAPTER 35

Participant: *Caregiver*
Age: *36*
Gender: *Male*
City: *Bangalore*
Occupation: *Game designer*

Q1) Who is in your family/friend suffering from?

Answer: My mother has been diagnosed with Schizophrenia.

Q2) How did you get to know about it, is there any story you want to share?

Answer: My mother was initially roughly diagnosed in approximately 2011. However, we really did not understand or take the diagnosis seriously. Eventually, she was clinically diagnosed in 2015 and has been on medication and care ever since.

The problem with mental illnesses is that they tend to be hard to be able to identify. They often manifest as other normally accepted human behaviour like rebellion, lack of personal hygiene, indisciplined behaviour or mood swings. It takes some effort from the caregivers to understand and identify the signs and be able to act accordingly.

Q3) How long has it been?

Answer: My mother has been under treatment since 2015. However, there is no actual date which we can identify as a trigger for the mental illness as it has slowly progressed over the years based on different events of trauma, etc.

Q4) Is s/he on medication?

Answer: Yes, she has been on regular medication since 2015. Medication is an absolute must and cannot be removed from the treatment.

Q5) How is it affecting your life?

Answer: Well, dealing with a loved one suffering from mental illness is one of the hardest, if not the hardest things, you might have to do. There has been a huge paradigm shift in the way I have had to think about and deal with my day to day life. For e.g., I have to be extra careful about my mother's safety and monitor it 24/7 as she cannot be allowed to travel on her own, or go out shopping, etc.

I have to be extra sensitive to her emotional needs and the things I say. For e.g., if I get upset with her and end up shouting at her, she will feel disproportionately guilty and this triggers suicidal thoughts in her. Therefore, I have to be careful with my words and cannot take her emotions for granted.

Q6) How is your work life?

Answer: My work life now has shifted to a work-from-home setup which works for me. This way I have been able to devote more time and energy to caring for my mother and even though my decision to work from home was not directly influenced by my mother's illness, it definitely helps me be more available to her and also be able to monitor her during the day.

Q7) What do you know about the challenges s/he faces?

Answer: I do not think I can completely understand what she goes through. Prior to treatment, my mother would hear voices and interpret those sounds and noises as voices speaking to her. This is something that used to frustrate me and I was not able to understand it. However, it has been a deep learning influence to not doubt what she says and accept that she was speaking the truth when she said she heard voices because she actually. The best we can do is try and empathise with what people who suffer from mental illnesses go through and try to be more sensitive and careful in trying to understand and believe them. The one thing that helped us the most was when I started trusting and believing what she told me instead of shouting at her or dismissing her struggles.

Q8) Do you want to convey any particular message to the community?

Answer: Yes, unfortunately in our society today we look down upon mental illnesses while mocking, making fun of and dismissing it. The words used in our vocabulary like "mad", "mental person", "crazy", etc do not at all sensitise us to the nuances of mental illnesses. People suffering from mental illnesses are like any other people suffering from other illnesses. They are no different from a person suffering from diabetes or a person suffering from cancer. The way most illnesses have a chemical reason, the same is true for mental illnesses which stem from a chemical imbalance in the brain where a certain chemical is not being produced correctly. Because the brain is also an organ like our other organs.

People suffering from mental illnesses are not dumb, or idiots. In fact, their logic and knowledge etc can be way better than normally functioning people. My mother has a knack for remembering the birthdays of all our friends and family members or even of celebrities. She is a math genius and a highly intelligent person. So we all need to treat people suffering with mental illnesses as normal patients like we would a friend or family suffering from blood pressure or diabetes etc and in that way, we can be more sensitive. Be kind and be loving. Love goes a long way in helping patients with mental illnesses.

Q9) What do you think that psychology as a sector needs to develop?

Answer: Psychology needs to catch up to the rest of the medical fraternity in terms of understanding the brain better and being able to develop new methods of treatment. There seems to be a huge lack of researched solutions and treatments for mental illnesses. There needs to be a more sensitised approach to educating all people on the various aspects of psychology and mental illnesses. Also, since the brain is a complicated organ, there have to be more creative ways of studying the brain and innovation needs to be a driving factor. I have seen things like simple video games and puzzles help my mother in her day to day life. It keeps her active and interested and creates a nice feedback and reward loop as well that helps. So using tools like entertainment and education to come up with creative ways of educating people as well as treating mental illnesses has to be the focus over the next few years.

Q10) Do you have any creative things that s/he has written and you want it to get published?

Answer: Nope.

CHAPTER 36

Participant: *Mentally ill*
Age: *62 years*
Gender: *Male*
City: *Mumbai*
Occupation: *Unemployed*

Q1) What are you suffering from?

Answer: I am suffering from BPAD-1 with the last few years being psychotic.

Q2) How did you get to know about it, is there any story you want to share?

Answer: Shivani, I was diagnosed with BPAD as late as when i was 57 years, after seeing almost 7 to 8 psychiatrists, I started to have Bipolar symptoms as early as when i was 14 years, so there is a big history of full blown mania with long bouts of depression. I have lost everything, my property, my family, everything I had.

Q3) How long has it been?

Answer: It's almost 48 years now.

Q4) Are you on medication?

Answer: No.

Q5) How is it affecting your life?

Answer: There is no life, each day is a struggle. I have no job, no money, nobody to ask.

Q6) What do you think that ordered people don't understand?

Answer: They don't understand anything and they don't want to. They think being manic is a habit and being depressed is being lazy.

Q7) Do you want to convey any particular message to the ordered people?

Answer: Not only other people but even psychiatrists, they should explain to the family about the disease and the family members should have understanding of what the person in going through.

Q8) What do you think that psychology as a sector needs to develop?

Answer: Psychology in India is still in its infant stage, first of all there are not enough psychiatrists in our country, where the ratio of mental health is much more higher than any other country, secondly even the psychiatrists who are available do not give enough time to the patient, My last psychiatrist who diagnosed my bipolar would hardly spend more than 10 minutes in a session, also the word mental health is still a taboo word in our country, if you are seeing a psychiatrist or a therapist it means either you are mad or totally loony, Mental health needs to be educated to the masses in a big way.

Q9) Do you have any creative things that you have written and you want it to get published?

Answer: I am looking for a shadow writer, I have the outline, but I am not motivated enough, because of my age and condition, otherwise I have done more than 6 years research on bi polar and have done live interviews with people suffering from Bipolar all over the world.

CHAPTER 37

Participant: *Mentally ill*
Age: *27 years*
Gender: *Female*
City: *Mumbai*
Occupation: *Customer experience & design consultant*

Q1) What are you suffering from?

Answer: Bipolar disorder 1.

Q2) How did you get to know about it, is there any story you want to share?

Answer: Started going for therapy and she identified the pattern in behaviour after which I went to a psychiatrist. He explained multiple disorders and observed too, after 2 months of visits it got diagnosed.

Q3) How long has it been?

Answer: 9 months.

Q4) Are you on medication?

Answer: Yes 3 mood stabilizers.

Q5) How is it affecting your life?

Answer: Affects my capacity to be reliable and maintain consistency at work and with my personal relationships.

Q6) How is your work life?

Answer: Office is really hectic and the stress triggers episodes at times.

Q7) What do you think that ordered people don't understand?

Answer: They need to be sensitized and aware of what BPAD is, and some basic measures of how to deal with a person who has it (similar to physically disabled people and instructions like sign language etc).

Q8) Do you want to convey any particular message to the ordered people?

Answer: It's a chronic disease just like diabetes, hypertension and is not the personality of the person, give them a chance and let the medication and therapy do its magic.

Q9) What do you think that psychology as a sector needs to develop?

Answer: Spread awareness beyond just taking care of mental health. Along with that specially for BPAD show the neurological and scientific explanation of why it occurs (the imbalance of dopamine serotonin norepinephrine in the brain etc).

Q10) Do you have any creative things that you have written and you want it to get published?

Answer: I used to be confused by my own behaviour as a teenager between manic and depressive episodes when I had a normal phase, back when I didn't even know I had bipolar disorder, and made self portraits expressing duality.

CHAPTER 38

Participant: *Mentally ill*
Age: *34 years*
Gender: *Male*
City: *Hyderabad*
Occupation: *Job in BPO sector*

Q1) What are you suffering from?

Answer: Bipolar disorder 1.

Q2) How did you get to know about it, is there any story you want to share?

Answer: I got to know it from the psychiatrist. Before that I suffered from bipolar disorder in my mid teens and didn't know what it was. I knew something was wrong with my mind but I couldn't say anything about it to any of my family members...I thought it was my own psychological defect as I cycled through depression and mania on day to day basis.....I thought that when I had mania I can do anything but when I had depression...I was helpless and didn't have a clue. It was after two years of suffering with this that I had my full blown mania where my family members realised that something was wrong and took me to some spiritual guy that we used to go for any issues. Because mania has some spiritual tendencies where you believe that you are a Messiah and are here to save the world. I was having a delusion that I'm Jesus Christ. It is because in my religion it is thought that Jesus is the one who will come to protect the world from sinners. So accordingly my behaviour manifested with this delusion. At that time...it felt like everything is a sign from God. Thankfully the spiritual guru admitted that he couldn't do anything and it was then that I was taken to psychiatrist where I was given drugs for sleep. I got into mania several times after that and was taken to psychiatrist several times which helped my shrink to diagnose me with bipolar disorder 1.

Q3) How long has it been?

Answer: 18 years.

Q4) Are you on medication?

Answer: Yes.

Q5) How is it affecting your life?

Answer: It affects every second of my life...I'm always thinking about my illness and how to overcome it. I have obsessive compulsive personality disorder as well which makes me have a tendency of perfection so I'm never happy with what I do and always introspect whatever I do on top of cognitive distortion. I'm not social and cannot communicate with people as I don't understand or stay confused with whatever they are talking.

Q6) How is your work life?

Answer: I left many jobs when I'm manic. When I'm manic I have big dreams which make me leave jobs in search of that elusive manic delusional goal.

Q7) What do you think that ordered people don't understand?

Answer: They don't know the extent to which we suffer and they think that if we are taking meds then we are 100 percent fine.

Q8) Do you want to convey any particular message to the ordered people?

Answer: It's hard for us to convey how we feel but please be patient when dealing with people with mental illness.

Q9) What do you think that psychology as a sector needs to develop?

Answer: Make mentally challenged people to be more inclusive in the society and spread awareness to avoid mistreatment of mentally challenged people.

Q10) Do you have any creative things that you have written and you want it to get published?

Answer: Nothing.

CHAPTER 39

Participant: *Mentally ill*
Age: *29*
Gender: *Male*
City: *Kolkata*
Occupation: *Entrepreneur*

Q1) What are you suffering from?

Answer: Bipolar disorder type 1.

Q2) How did you get to know about it, is there any story you want to share?

Answer: At first there were depressive episodes, then came the manic episode through which i knew.

Q3) How long has it been?

Answer: About 13 years onset and 7 years since diagnosis of bipolar.

Q4) Are you on medication?

Answer: Yes.

Q5) How is it affecting your life?

Answer: I sleep more than usual, work slow, had one break up so i don't know if it is due to lack of therapies or lack of understanding from the other side. There is a lot of stigma attached to it. Not many people are sensitised or tend to understand. There is a lack of awareness.

Q6) How is your work life?

Answer: Just started work.

Q7) What do you think that ordered people don't understand?

Answer: Most of them don't wanna admit or understand that mental illness even exists and its suffering is real .

Q8) Do you want to convey any particular message to the ordered people?

Answer: Get awareness, accept that mental illness, anxiety,panic, depression is real and its suffering is real. not something to be snapped out of and its not all in the mind.

Q9) What do you think that psychology as a sector needs to develop?

Answer: I believe the number of psychiatrists and psychologists need to increase and doctor to patient ratio needs to improve. MHCA 2017 needs to be implemented by respective states to open hospitals, shelter homes, community centres to accommodate mentally ill people. Two biggest sectors that need improvement are marriage and career among mentally ill that need attention. These two places are the places where they suffer lot of discrimination and stigma. This needs to change.

Q10) Do you have any creative things that you have written and you want it to get published?

Answer: I once wrote love notes to my ex girlfriend, don't know if it qualifies for something creative. But in future i dream of writing a book.

CHAPTER 40

Participant: *Caregiver*
Age: *34*
Gender: *Female*
City: *NCR*
Occupation: *Psychologist*

Q1) Who is in your family/friend suffering from?

Answer: Spouse diagnosed with Bipolar Affective Disorder.

Q2) How did you get to know about it, is there any story you want to share?

Answer: I knew about it before getting married to him, but for the duration I knew no episode visibly occurred. However, I witnessed an episode two weeks into our marriage when Manic with Psychosis occurred. It is surely important to note that he was first diagnosed when psychotic symptoms were observed by friends and family, after a get-together where his friends offered him marijuana when they were all already drinking alcohol. While the second episode of mania did not involve any substance abuse.

Q3) How long has it been?

Answer: He was first diagnosed in 2007-2008.

Q4) Is s/he on medication?

Answer: For over two years he has been on regular medication, except for a few misses here and there.

Q5) How is it affecting your life?

Answer: Since our marriage, we have observed some rapid cycling and mostly depressive episodes. During the transitions he had made some impulsive financial and career decisions which had impacted our finances and having incurred a lot of debt. I struggled with postpartum depression due to financial crises we went through around the birth of our child.

Q6) How is your work life?

Answer: I have for most duration since marriage been a freelance Psychologist. I work from home based office and take limited no of sessions per day/week so I can manage my personal life well.

Q7) What do you know about the challenges s/he faces?

Answer: He has had initial difficulty with handling negative and intrusive thoughts, extreme outbursts of anger in which he hit himself and broke things. The swings in mood lead to physical fatigue and he has had difficulty finding motivation in the past. However, with regular medication and self empowerment, he has learned to identify his emotions better, and learned to control his impulses at large. He also periodically dealt with a lot of guilt after having taken the reckless financial/career decision which led to the whole family struggling in the past.

Q8) Do you want to convey any particular message to the community?

Answer: People with psychological disorders are as productive and successful as their environment reflects. So before blaming or shaming them look at how you or others around them are. With appropriate measures (medication, therapy, family support and social acceptance), they can live as functional life as most people.

Q9) What do you think that psychology as a sector needs to develop?

Answer: Psychology as a profession is not only a science but also art. While the education system does offer a arts degree in psychology, mostly the scientific methodology is only emphasized upon. Thus we get more technically trained professionals who lack the sensitivity required by the profession. Having said that, I think we need better structuring in the field of Psychology where art and science degrees in psychology have clear distinction and for being a therapist focus is more on having qualities of empathy and compassion in the professionals than researching. Clinical psychologists may not always be the best therapists and not all effective therapists have a higher degree in clinical psychology. Academic and therapeutic processes require different innate skills and the policy makers need to take this into consideration, as we as a nation tops the list of the most depressed nations.

Q10) Do you have any creative things that s/he has written and you want it to get published?

Answer: My spouse paints.

Analysis

Compiling interviews on mental health into a book was not an easy task. There are many misconceptions about mental health. We have been taught that a mentally ill person is likely to end up in an isolation ward or mental asylum. Indians are often afraid to be identified as a mentally ill person because of the stigma associated with mental disorders in our society. In the Hindi language there are no words explaining mental illness. Unfortunately there is only one negative and inappropriate word which is widely used - MAD.

I personally strongly disagree with this attitude towards mentally ill people. This is the main reason for this compilation of interviews of mentally ill people and caregivers, so that we can understand what exactly they are thinking and facing in reality. It is not an easy task for sufferers to come forward and share their personal and challenging insights. Some were able to pour their hearts out while others were constrained, perhaps fearing who would read their story. Yes, people are afraid to share because of the associated stigma. I want everyone to see that people with mental illness are not unintelligent and they deserve the same respect and treatment in the community just like any person.

I am highlighting a few points below which I observed throughout these interviews:

- These interviews reveal that taking medicine for your mental wellbeing is not wrong

- After decades people are still unaware about their mental illness and its impact on daily life
- People are willing to come forward and share their story but fear societies lack of acceptance of mentally ill people
- People with mental illness are looking for empathy not sympathy
- Self education and self analysis can greatly improve your life
- Mental illness and intelligence are two different things
- Mentally ill and mentally retarded or challenged are not the same
- Mentally ill people's thoughts and ambitions are similar to ordered people
- Where there is a will, there is a way
- Mentally ill people can lead a normal life like getting married or having children
- With age people with a mental illness can become more independent
- In 2020 people still treat mentally ill people as though they are 'faking' their illness or hiding at home to avoid work
- We should not associate mentally ill people with being weak
- People taking medicines for many years and are capable of managing their wellbeing
- People with mental illness can work hard and live a normal life, however their routine needs to be adjusted to the surroundings which can make all the difference to themselves and their families' experience
- All the participants in the book are knowledgeable and educated about mental illness. They articulated that we need to focus on changing methods of counseling, awareness campaigns and for society to learn to be more empathetic.

A Note from Shivani Thapliyal: Life and Mental Health Coach

My journey started when I started seeing and listening to an unknown identity which was not there. It followed me my whole life. I was a kid so I thought if I have the power to interact with other dimensions that means I am not a normal human being, I am a supernatural being. I grew up with this thought in my mind and never shared it with anyone. My teenage years were fine because I always slept with my parents but as an adult it manifested in a new way. I was not prepared for the hardships that were about to come my way, partly because everything with me seemed normal to other people. I felt an energy in me become stronger and I became aware of a presence surrounding me. I developed insomnia and started taking sleeping pills from the very young age of 17. I never knew why but I have always felt a fear at night. When I started my career, everything was going fine. I relocated to Mumbai from a small city and at that time my college supported me because they could see my enthusiasm to change and to do something with my life. I first tried acting but after a year I realised that this was not for me, so I started working off camera just to survive. At this point things were getting confused in my mind but I was not conscious of it. People started distancing themselves from me when they learned about my self harm behaviour when I was feeling hurt. I was working hard but without any specific aim in life. I worked conscientiously but I was dissatisfied. Things worsened when my career grew and my stress level and responsibilities increased. I started losing weight and became absent minded. As a result I resigned from my job because I was unable to concentrate. I wanted to do something else, but unfortunately things didn't work out as I had hoped.

But you never know where the future is going to lead you. I consulted a few psychiatrists and I learned that I was suffering from a mental illness. It was explained that I have chemical imbalance in my brain which affects my reality. I was given medication and at first I was confused, I wasn't sure how to let go of my previous beliefs. I came across a peer support group created by Vijay Nallawala, the founder of Bipolar India, and from there I received the motivation to improve my life. During my journey I have realised that there is always a reason behind something, you just need to wait and see what unfolds. Today I am very thankful that I have been through these tough times because it has given me the ability to empathise with other people's pain.

I received my REBT (Rational Emotive Behavioral Therapy) Mindset Life Coach certification in 2019. I chose this career because I want to help people in making good choices in life, and assist them to become as independent as possible. I want to make people aware that mentally ill people are not stupid and anybody can be trained. It is a matter of your will power and desires and needs. I also want to become a pillar for those people with mental illness who need to know someone understands their life challenges, and that they are not alone!

This has been my journey of how I came to be a life and mental health coach, and now it has become part of my life.

www.ingramcontent.com/pod-product-compliance
Lightning Source LLC
Chambersburg PA
CBHW020720160726

47993CB00006B/2276